block parties & poker nights

block parties & poker nights

Recipes and Ideas for Getting and Staying Connected with Your Neighbors

peggy allen

clarkson potter/publishers

new york

Published by Clarkson Potter/Publishers, New York, New York.
Member of the Crown Publishing Group, a division of Random House, Inc.
www.randomhouse.com

CLARKSON N. POTTER is a trademark and POTTER and colophon are registered trademarks of Random House, Inc.

Printed in the United States of America

Design by Jan Derevjanik

Library of Congress Cataloging-in-Publication Data

Allen, Peggy.
Block parties and poker nights : recipes and ideas for getting and staying connected with your neighbors / Peggy Allen. — 1st ed.
1. Cookery. 2. Entertaining. I. Title.
TX714 .A452 2002
642′.2 — dc21   2002025236

ISBN 0-609-80788-9

10 9 8 7 6 5 4 3 2 1

First Edition

To my parents, Jack and Lorry Lambert,
who have always taught by example.

acknowledgments

I have been extremely fortunate to have met women who have become good, great, dear friends. Some were neighbors, some coworkers, some childhood pals. Along with my brothers and sisters, sisters-in-law, mom, and mom's chums, they were extremely generous with their time and their own neighborhood stories, and they are all responsible for most of this book. To each I am grateful. I'd like to thank Susie Taylor; Adrienne Hammel; Jean Kagan; Linda Eckhardt; my agent, Richard Henshaw; my editor, Pam Krauss; Heidi Diamond, who pointed me in the right direction; and Lisa Nee, my business partner and friend. Thanks to Paula Cohen for her delightful illustrations. Finally I extend my love and appreciation to my husband, Todd, and our daughters, Lori and Katie, who complete my world wherever we live.

contents

introduction

Some best friends for life came together because of a purchase my husband, Todd, made while we were vacationing in Key West. He came home from the Jimmy Buffett store with a postcard featuring a recipe for margaritas. There were ingredients on the list that I had never heard of, and when he made the first batch, I thought it looked like someone's pool water. Fortunately, it tasted quite a bit better.

One Sunday, shortly after returning from our Florida trip, we were watching our toddler riding her tricycle at the end of the driveway. Todd mentioned his new recipe to a neighbor we knew only slightly, and the next thing I knew, the guy and his toddler were in our yard and Todd was mixing up a pitcher. Within a matter of weeks word had spread, and we found ourselves making batches of margaritas and hosting a crew of adults, all with small kids in tow, each Sunday night. We started rotating houses and sharing cocktails, finger food, and a couple of hours of conversation while the kids played (or, in some cases, destroyed our houses) and ate hot dogs. What a scene—and what fun. We met each Sunday (save holidays) for nearly four straight years. Our kids grew up together, and so did the adults. Somewhere along the line, we came to refer to our weekly gatherings as Sundowners, as the original Key West celebrants did. And though we have since all moved to different neighborhoods, towns, and states, we still stay in close touch and the kids remain good friends.

A lot of people talk about neighborhood as a thing of the past, something we associate with old sitcoms and times when life was easier, simpler. There's good reason for that. Many of us did grow up in wonderful, active neighborhoods where the moms stayed home while the dads went off to work. I myself grew up in a large patchwork of homes where everyone's backyard seemed to overlap everyone else's. The houses were all different sizes, some brand new, some ancient, and there was always a pack of dogs and kids of all ages. I spent summers scooting through hedges, hooting calls to find out who was around to play, and inventing group games to fill the days. At the time, I took the fact that there were kids to play with for granted, and I was oblivious of the friendships my mother was building. Not until I had left home and started making my own tentative steps toward building a community, a place I could call home, did I realize those neighbors had been my mother's best friends. I found I had learned much from her, without knowing it, about building enduring friendships. My mother and her group set great examples and showed that in a *real* neighborhood, there are certain givens: You can count on people to look after you. You can count on people to look after your property. You can count on people to care about your family almost as much as you do, and almost as much as they care about their *own* families. And you can always count on someone to show up with a pot of soup or a plate of brownies just when you need them most; it was just understood that we all nurtured one another in ways big and small.

What turns a cluster of houses or a street of brownstones into a neighborhood? I began to think about the answer shortly after a recent neighborhood progressive dinner party. I was determined to set up the house to accommodate thirty-two for a sit-down meal. Cheri Allen called to offer her help—what did I need? Several trips later, Cheri's lawn chairs and silverware were arranged in my living room. It was a bit of a mishmash from a decorating point of view, but without those old lawn chairs, I couldn't have seated everyone. And ultimately, it's not how you present yourself and your home that matters; it's spending time together and putting in the effort required to make sure everyone is included and comfortable.

Over the years I've found there are few more relaxed ways to get acquainted (or catch up) than over a meal. Food is a common language we all speak, and it's a nonthreatening, very relatable way for us to share some of our cultural background, as well. And hey, we all have to eat, right?

Beyond that, offering food instantly puts folks at ease because it gives your event a focal point that *everyone* can participate in and perhaps even contribute to. No worries about standing around idly when there's a buffet to peruse or burgers to flip. And while a new neighbor may feel awkward about accepting your offer to baby-sit or unpack china, only a true recluse would not be grateful to find a batch of scones or pot of stew on the doorstep. A gift of food is also a great excuse if *you're* the one who is not entirely comfortable marching through the hedges with your hand extended to meet strangers.

For some people meeting and fitting in is second nature, and they can carry on a conversation with just about anyone. I envy their facility, but for most of us, it takes a level of comfort to reach out and initiate a conversation—much less a block party or streetwide cleanup. This book is intended to help you achieve that level of comfort and inspire some first, second, and third steps. All the people in the book are real, and their stories are as true to their worlds as yours will be to your own unique and special neighborhood. Their events are all different, but they share three vital elements: They are nonthreatening, easy to say yes to, and free of cliques. And of course, everybody eats well.

As for the recipes, let me be honest: I'm a fair-weather cook. Some months I'll cook every day; other times it's steaks on the grill and store-bought desserts. But when it comes to our neighborhood events, I'll always invest the effort to put together something that shows I care—and elicits requests for the recipe. Over the years I've collected some home runs that I can share with confidence. Many of those who told their stories also shared their neighborhood favorites, and to them I am very grateful. The key to many of the dishes in this book is that they travel well, they are easy to reheat, and they're all crowd-pleasers. Share them with someone you want to know better, and they will taste even better.

When I began interviewing people about their neighborhoods and their experiences as neighbors, I was thrilled to learn all the diverse, clever, and original ideas that people pursue in order to build and sustain their neighborhoods. It's clear from all the conversations I've had that people have fun, but what seems even more rewarding is the old two-plus-two-makes-five side to it; the reward is greater than the sum of the parts. People come away feeling connected, more grounded, hopeful, and genuinely happy. When you feel part of a neighborhood, you will find day-to-day living much more enjoyable, guaranteed.

Of course, as with most things, getting started is the hardest part. It is so easy not to pick up the phone, not to stop and toss a newspaper up on a porch, not to stop long enough to visit with someone who's in the yard raking, shoveling, planting, or painting. Know that the rewards more than justify the extra effort, and along the way, you and your new friends will eat like kings!

block parties & poker nights

breaking the ice

When my husband and I moved from the New York area to the Midwest, it meant a lot of changes for the whole family. We left behind a house I thought I would grow old in and a neighborhood loaded with good people and great memories. I spent the first few days unpacking and fighting back tears. But after a week of feeling sorry for myself I was ready to get the lay of the new land. I took advantage of the warm weather, putting in hours in the garden in front of my house

Welcome Gifts

Adele's Pecans 8

Pungent Peanuts 9

Garlic Olives 10

Sunflower Nibbles 11

Jean's Dill-and-Garlic Vinegar 12

Strawberry Jam 13

Pat's Garden Salsa 16

Hot Fudge Sauce 17

Classic Pesto 18

Play Dough 19

Banana Bread 20

Cocktail Meet-and-Greet

Bubblin' Artichoke Dip 30

Stuffed Cucumber Wheels 31

Cocktail Potato Pancakes 32

Deviled Crab 34

Shrimp Dip 35

Prosciutto-and-Gruyère Pinwheels 36

Crabmeat-and-Shrimp Surprise 37

Breakfast Get-Together

Orange-Scented Scones 22

Almond or Hazelnut Biscotti 23

Apricot Nut Cake 25

Hills' Blueberry Cake 26

Raisin Bread French Toast 27

Fruit Salad with Honey French
Dressing 28

Ladies' Luncheon

The Busy Ladies' Lunch Soup 39

American Blue Cheese Dressing 40

Creamy Yogurt-Mustard Dressing 41

Herb Garlic Croutons 42

and walking my dog often. One by one, I met people in the neighborhood. Slowly I began the inevitable mental shift that occurs when you stop thinking house and start thinking *home.* I got names straight. Neighbors stopped in with gifts, lists, and an invitation to a dinner party soon followed.

Whether you've just moved into a new neighborhood or you're a longtime resident who wishes your area felt more connected, there are countless ways, both large and small, to help foster a cohesive community. Chances are, if you'd like to have a stronger connection to your neighbors, they would, too. But someone has to take the first step. Why not be the one who extends the dinner party invitation to *your* new neighbors?

Here are some things to bear in mind:

◆ Stay open to differences. Getting to know your neighbors means opening your circle to a wide range of people. Recognize the age diversity in your own area. You may hope for neighbors who have kids the same age as yours, but I've learned the most about what's around the corner for my own kids through sidewalk chats and deep conversations with parents of older kids. They have provided invaluable insight into the social and school-related issues that my kids will face. The lesson here — every house and every neighbor has much to contribute to the rich tapestry of your neighborhood. You'll never know just what it is, however, unless you take the leap and get acquainted.

◆ Don't just target people with whom you think you have the most in common. I once was asked to go to a neighbor's house to pick up an entrée she had prepared for a soup kitchen. This older woman with grandchildren lived a few blocks away, and I had never before had the occasion to meet her. When I rang the doorbell she called out that I should come right in. I did, and what a wonderful treat I encountered. Spread out in her living room, the beginnings of a handmade quilt occupied the entire floor. It was as colorful and complicated as could be, and even a complete quilting novice like me knew I was in the presence of a gifted artisan. Cathie Staley and I talked for quite some time about her quilting and her family. She showed me photos of quilts she had made for others and gave me great tips for my own quilting projects. It was inspiring. After that day I enjoyed frequent visits and borrowed quilting books from her often.

◆ Remember how you felt when you were the newcomer and make the first move. Stop by with a welcome basket of goodies, including something for exhausted parents (a bottle of wine), something for homesick kids (a batch of homemade play dough), and the promise of a play date or free baby-sitting. Drop off a neighborhood directory and a simple chicken dinner. Bundle together takeout menus from your favorite delivery joints with a video from your favorite rental place, a bag of microwave popcorn, and a few dozen of your most decadent cookies.

If you're not comfortable with a one-on-one approach, don't let that stop you from reaching out. Many neighborhoods hold annual or less predictably scheduled get-to-know-you events that enable newcomers to meet the old guard in a casual setting. This has the advantage of introducing the new arrival to lots of folks at one time, and spreads the responsibility for keeping them engaged in conversation among several people. Just be certain if you do invite new members of the community into your circle that your primary goal is to help them put some names, faces, and family histories together. So don't get too caught up in your own visiting to notice if someone is between chats.

In this chapter I've written about three good excuses for gathering up the neighborhood to welcome new neighbors and greet old ones: morning coffee, welcome-to-the-neighborhood cocktail party, and the "very busy ladies' luncheon" started by an old friend of mine. I hope these and several other ideas will motivate you to try something that you think will work in your area.

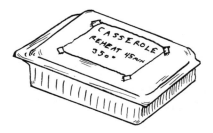

a welcome gift

Two weeks after we had moved into our home in Wilmette, Illinois, I received a call around six o'clock. It was a neighbor saying her son was on his way over with dinner. Minutes later, this young man walked through our back hedge with a roast chicken on a platter with a salad and some brownies. Having spent the day trying to get my daughters registered for classes, I thought this was a gift from heaven.

Whether you choose to cook something or purchase it, dropping off food, spirits, or a basket of housewarming items is a lovely idea. Consider making the deliveries on a weekend when both you and your new neighbor might have a little more time for a short chat. Don't count on their remembering all your vital statistics. Write your name, address, and phone number on whatever you bring by. Avoid including anything that must be returned; disposable or inexpensive giveaway containers are best.

New neighbors have a lot on their minds. If they don't jump out the door to say hello, don't assume that they're stiffs or stuck-up. Families are often swamped just getting settled in a new home. Anything you can do to let a neighbor know you're there and available to help out will be appreciated, trust me.

Here are some ideas about what to bring:

- A basket of local produce and a card explaining where it came from
- A kit containing a local map, the What's Where community resource list (see page 43), a local phone book
- Takeout menus
- The local paper (It took me three weeks to figure out that everyone relied on one particular local paper for all the community information.)
- An invitation to the next neighborhood gathering, no matter how far off it is
- A simple, family-style dinner, like chicken, a stew, or a baked pasta dish. Include some paper plates, napkins, and forks—along with some cups and a container of iced tea.

ADELE'S PECANS

adele's pecans

makes 1 pound

Adele Wolfe shared the recipe for this New Orleans favorite. These are very hard to part with.

4 tablespoons (½ stick) butter

1 pound pecan halves

1 tablespoon salt

½ teaspoon white pepper

Preheat the oven to 350°F. Melt the butter in a cookie sheet with sides. Stir in the pecans, and coat them well. Bake for 20 minutes, stirring every 5 minutes.

Sprinkle the pecans with the salt and white pepper and let them cool in the pan; store them in an airtight container.

make a welcome gift

If you have time, a homemade gift feels more personal and sets a tone of real sharing right from the start. You just can't go wrong with the following recipes. Package one up in a fun container and you're set.

PUNGENT PEANUTS

pungent
peanuts

makes 2 pounds

An easy gift from your kitchen, these peanuts keep well.

Corn or peanut oil for deep-frying
(plus 1 1/2 cups)

2 pounds shelled and skinned raw peanuts

6 heads fresh garlic, individual cloves
peeled and sliced

Hickory-seasoned celery salt

Heat 2 to 3 inches of oil in a deep, heavy pot or wok until almost smoking. Deep-fry the peanuts in several batches on medium-high heat, stirring constantly. Be careful not to let the peanuts burn.

As the nuts begin to brown, turn down the heat and continue to cook until they're light golden brown. Remove the nuts and drain on plates stacked with paper towels. Let the peanuts cool while you fry the remaining batches.

Heat the 1 1/2 cups of oil in a heavy skillet on medium-high heat. Add the sliced garlic, stirring constantly to prevent burning. As the garlic browns, reduce the heat and continue to stir, cooking until the garlic is crisp and light golden.

Remove the cooked garlic with a strainer and drain on paper towels, breaking up any clusters. When cool, combine the garlic with the peanuts, and salt to taste. Store this treat in airtight containers.

GARLIC OLIVES

makes 2 cups

You can vary the herbs as you like, or add strips of citrus peel or dried pepper flakes.

> 2 cups drained pitted black olives
>
> 2 tablespoons extra virgin olive oil
>
> 2 large garlic cloves, minced (1 1/2 teaspoons)
>
> 1/2 teaspoon dried oregano

Toss the olives with the oil, garlic, and oregano. Marinate in a closed container for 4 hours or longer in the refrigerator. The longer you marinate the olives, the more pungent their flavor.

You know it's a neighborhood when

Everyone has keys to your house

Some people even have keys to your car

House-sitting goes without saying

No one objects when kids in bathing suits run through all the sprinklers

The hedges have gaps — on purpose

SUNFLOWER NIBBLES

sunflower nibbles

makes 2 cups

Smoky-tasting and addictive, these may replace popcorn as a movie snack at your house.

 1 tablespoon olive oil

 2 cups shelled raw sunflower seeds

 8 garlic cloves, minced (4 teaspoons)

 $1/4$ teaspoon salt

 1 teaspoon hickory smoke seasoning or 1 tablespoon soy sauce

Heat the oil in a large frying pan on medium-high heat. Add the sunflower seeds and garlic. Stir. When the seeds begin to change color, reduce the heat to medium and continue stirring until about half the seeds are lightly browned, less than 5 minutes.

Remove the seeds from the heat, and add salt to taste. After 5 minutes, when the sunflower seeds begin to cool, add the hickory seasoning or soy sauce and stir well. Allow the seeds to cool completely; then store them in a tightly covered jar or tin.

JEAN'S DILL

- AND -

GARLIC VINEGAR

This is a very good condiment for those on low-salt diets. You'll need to find dill that's in flower, which is easy if you have an herb garden. Otherwise, head to the farmer's market.

6 very fresh garlic cloves, peeled and slightly mashed

6 to 8 heads fresh dill, with flowers

1 quart white wine vinegar

Place the garlic in a clean quart jar. Pack the dill upside down on top of the garlic. Fill the jar with vinegar.

Seal the jar tightly and put it in the pantry or in a dark area for 1 month. Strain the liquid, and pour it into an attractive bottle. Cork the bottle and tie with raffia or ribbon. Discard the garlic and dill.

STRAWBERRY JAM

When the strawberries are at their ripest, clear out a Saturday afternoon and be prepared for sweet smells and a little heat in the kitchen. The pectin box says you shouldn't make double batches, but I've had no trouble doubling this recipe. The key is to measure precisely.

- 2 quarts ripe, fresh strawberries
- 7 cups sugar
- 1 box of Sure-jell fruit pectin

Wash eight 8-ounce jars with 2-piece lids in soap and water and rinse completely. Put the lids in a pan and cover with boiling water and leave until ready to use.

Wash and hull the strawberries. Place 1 quart at a time in the food processor and pulse until crushed; don't overprocess. You should have 5 cups of crushed strawberries. Place them in a 6- to 8-quart saucepan. Premeasure the sugar and set it aside. Stir the pectin into the fruit and bring the mixture to a full rolling boil on high heat, stirring constantly.

Stir in the sugar all at once and return the mixture to a full rolling boil. Boil for exactly 1 minute, stirring constantly, then remove from the heat. Use a large metal mixing spoon to skim off any foam.

Ladle the mixture into the prepared jars, filling each to within ⅛ inch of the tops. Wipe the jar rim and threads clean. Cover with flat lids and screw bands on tightly. Turn the jars over for 5 minutes, then turn them upright. After the jars have cooled, check the seals by pressing the middle of the lid with your finger. If the lid pops up, it is not sealed. Store the sealed jars in a cool dry dark place for up to a year.

when you are the
new neighbor

Meeting new people is not always easy. Until you have experienced it, it's hard to explain how isolating being the newbie can feel and how long it takes to truly feel part of a neighborhood. Not all neighborhoods roll out the welcome mat right away, and often the demands of a new job, family, and settling in can slow down your own efforts to get acquainted. Here are some small things you can do to feel more acclimated—and a few brave things you can try if you're up to it.

- Don't make coffee. Go to the local coffee shop. If you make it a routine, you'll become a familiar face. Stay and read the paper if you have time. Weekends can be the best times to go.

- Join a church, synagogue, or mosque near your new home. Use the church directory to find out who lives near you, and volunteer your time to help out. This will help you to meet new people.

- Sit outside. My neighbor, Laurel Tyler, said that the best way she and her husband connected with their neighbors was by sitting on the stoop of her city apartment. "Our stairs were filled with neighbors every night!" Sitting on your steps invites people to stop, chat, and stay awhile.

- If you have children, use their school as a way to make connections by volunteering for cafeteria duty, the book fair, or playground patrol. Some schools draw from such a large area that you may feel you're meeting people from miles away, but it's a small world. Chances are you may meet people through school who'll introduce you to people right next door.

- If you have a dog, walk it often and at different times of day. Claire Murray lives in New York City, and she's become dear friends with her neighbors, all thanks to her dog, Speckles.

- Spring is a great time to meet people. Even if you're not keen on yard work, take it up. Nothing seems to invite a visit like lawn care or weeding. (If you're lucky, you won't get any work done!) A small garden in your front yard or a container garden on your doorstep gives neighbors common ground for conversation.

- Throw a party. My husband and I give a Kentucky Derby party every May, and it has become one of our favorite annual events. It's a great excuse to invite the entire neighborhood, including neighbors we barely know, into our home. New neighbors like it because they don't have to commit to a whole evening (the race is at 6:04 P.M. EST and is over in minutes) and it's a time of year when you're not competing with vacations, holidays, or gorgeous weather. Our betting system sees more and more action each year.

My friend Crystal Johns recently moved from her home of fourteen years to a new part of the country and was having a hard time meeting her neighbors. Few people had kids, and the individual properties were just big enough to make it hard to run into people. Crystal's solution was to invite her neighbors to a champagne brunch.

First, she put a list together of whom to invite and how many confirmations she needed to justify the event. She decided not to send out invitations; instead, she called to suggest possible dates. The toughest step was that first phone call. Crystal said the key was to be flexible and ask people to pencil in a date, so she could see if there were scheduling conflicts. Once she had enough people who could make the date, she called back to confirm.

PAT'S GARDEN SALSA

Bring a jar of this to a host or hostess. Mild or hot, it's a very nice gift that is good with pita or tortilla chips, in Mexican dips, on grilled meats, or on omelets.

1 pound plum tomatoes, cored and chopped

1/2 small red onion, finely diced

1 garlic clove, chopped, or more to taste

2 tablespoons fresh lime juice

2 tablespoons chopped cilantro or parsley

1 green bell pepper, diced

1/4 teaspoon salt

1 teaspoon chopped jalapeño pepper, or 3 or 4 dashes hot red pepper sauce, optional

Drain the chopped tomatoes in a colander, and then place them in a medium bowl. Stir in the onion, garlic, lime juice, cilantro, bell pepper, salt, and jalapeño pepper, if using.

Let the mixture stand at room temperature, covered, for 2 hours to blend the flavors. Ladle the salsa into nice jars, cover, and refrigerate for up to 1 week.

HOT FUDGE SAUCE

makes 1½ cups

If you know someone who is fond of ice cream sundaes, a jar of this rich sauce is a nice present indeed. Pair it with a few sundae glasses and a quart of ice cream for a fun move-in gift.

- 4 tablespoons (½ stick) unsalted butter
- 1 tablespoon cornstarch
- ¼ cup cocoa
- ½ cup honey
- ½ cup water
- Pinch of salt
- ½ teaspoon vanilla extract
- Handful of miniature marshmallows

Melt the butter in a small saucepan.

Add the cornstarch, cocoa, honey, and water, and stir until the mixture is thick. Remove the saucepan from the heat, and add the salt, vanilla, and marshmallows. Stir well, until the marshmallows melt.

Pour the sauce into a fancy small jar, cover, and refrigerate until you're ready to use it. This will keep for about 2 weeks in the refrigerator.

CLASSIC PESTO

Tried and true, pesto has so many uses. For a dip with punch, add sour cream (as much as you like) to the really garlicky variation. Or mix the pesto, to taste, with one pint of heavy cream, and layer it on cooked lasagna noodles with shredded Jack cheese for a yummy change of pace.

2 cups basil leaves, torn in pieces

1/2 cup extra virgin olive oil

2 tablespoons pine nuts

2 garlic cloves

1 teaspoon salt

1/2 cup grated Parmesan cheese

3 tablespoons melted butter

Combine the basil, olive oil, pine nuts, garlic, and salt in a blender, and blend until smooth. Transfer the mixture to a bowl, and stir in the Parmesan and melted butter. Cover the pesto and store it in the refrigerator for up to 1 week.

POWER PESTO

Increase the garlic to 5 cloves. Watch out—this is potent!

PLAY DOUGH

play
dough

makes 4 cups

Want to be a hit with the new kids on the block? Send over some play dough with a recipe—and have your little one deliver it.

2 cups flour

1 cup salt

4 teaspoons cream of tartar

2 cups water

$\frac{1}{4}$ cup vegetable oil

Food coloring of your choice

In a large skillet, combine the flour, salt, and cream of tartar. Make a well in the center of this mixture, and pour in the water, oil, and food coloring. Using a wooden spoon, stir the mixture over low heat until it thickens to the consistency of children's modeling clay. Cool the clay completely; then store it in an airtight plastic container.

BANANA BREAD

banana bread

makes 2 loaves

Comfort food, as familiar as your favorite slippers, this classic quick bread is a great way to say welcome. Lining the baking pans with waxed paper or parchment, though not essential, makes removing the finished loaves a snap.

$^1/_4$ pound plus 2 tablespoons ($1^1/_4$ sticks) butter

1 cup granulated sugar

$^2/_3$ cup packed light brown sugar

2 large eggs

$^2/_3$ cup milk

2 teaspoons white wine vinegar

$^1/_2$ teaspoon baking soda

$1^1/_4$ cups mashed banana

$2^1/_3$ cups flour

2 teaspoons baking powder

$^1/_2$ cup nuts

$^1/_2$ teaspoon salt

1 teaspoon vanilla extract

Dash of ground cinnamon

Preheat the oven to 350°F. Grease two 8 × 4–inch loaf pans or line them with waxed paper. In a large mixing bowl, combine the butter and sugars. Beat 1 egg at a time into the butter mixture.

Combine the milk with the vinegar in a mixing cup, and let it stand 2 minutes. Stir the baking soda into the milk. Add the milk mixture and banana to the bowl, and mix well. Stir in the flour and baking powder; then add the nuts, salt, vanilla, and cinnamon. Divide the batter evenly between 2 loaf pans. Bake until the bread is golden brown, about 35 minutes. Let the banana bread cool for a few minutes in the pans; then turn it out onto a rack to cool completely.

a neighborhood newsletter

Some large and very well organized neighborhoods have a newsletter to keep residents updated and informed. Creating a newsletter takes time and energy, but it may be something your neighborhood could really benefit from. I came across a terrific one from Victoria Estates, a subdivision outside of Atlanta, Georgia, with about 160 households. The newsletter is called "News, Views & Voices," and it comes out quarterly. It runs around eight pages, has a light, breezy tone, and is always packed with great information.

Here's a sample of what they include:

- Community Events Update—includes neighborhood-wide events and how to sign up to help with specific committee needs and chores. It also includes write-ups on recent successes.

- Neighborhood News—welcomes new neighbors and includes names, phone numbers, and addresses. This section also extends sympathy to families who have experienced a recent loss, as well as get-well news, weddings, births, and congratulations to recent college graduates, and finally, good-byes to folks who are moving.

- Speak Your Piece—this section offers neighbors a way to communicate directly to the community. One issue included a thank-you to all those who had begun to slow down and drive more safely through the neighborhood.

- Question & Answer Columns—taking advantage of local talent, the newsletter occasionally features a column by a doctor in the neighborhood who answers arcane medical history questions. One submitted a few years ago was, "What exactly is laetrile, and how did it get its reputation as a treatment for cancer?" Maybe there is a gardener, contractor, or gourmet cook in your area who could write a similar column.

- Neighbor Features—this section includes an assortment of neighborhood stories written by fellow residents.

orange-scented
scones

ORANGE-SCENTED SCONES

makes 8 scones

These scones make a great "welcome to the 'hood" gift in a nice tin. They are really delicious. Drop by a neighbor's house for tea with a batch of scones and some fancy tea bags, and I guarantee you'll be invited back soon.

1¾ cups all-purpose flour (or 1 cup organic bread flour plus ¾ cup organic pastry flour)

2 teaspoons baking powder

½ teaspoon kosher salt

1 tablespoon sugar

Grated zest of 1 medium orange

½ cup (1 stick) cold unsalted butter, cut into ⅓-inch cubes

⅔ cup buttermilk, plus additional for brushing onto scones

2 tablespoons Sugar in the Raw or additional granulated sugar

Preheat the oven to 400°F. Line a baking sheet with parchment paper, or grease the pan lightly.

Combine the flour, baking powder, salt, and sugar in an electric mixer. Using the paddle attachment, mix in the orange zest. Add the butter, and mix just until it is coated with flour. The butter chunks should remain fairly large—no less than half their original size. With the mixer set on low, add the ⅔ cup buttermilk, and mix until the liquid is just incorporated. Stop mixing when the dough begins to pull away from the sides of the bowl.

Scrape the dough from the bowl, and shape it into a ball. With well-floured fingers, pat the dough into a 7-inch disk. Cut the disk into quarters and then again into eighths. Set the scones on the baking sheet, and brush with the additional buttermilk. Sprinkle the scones with sugar, and bake them for 15 to 20 minutes, until browned.

ALMOND OR HAZELNUT biscotti BISCOTTI

This is Sally Hespe's signature treat. A plate of these go well with a bag of espresso or coffee beans.

$^1/_3$ cup butter or margarine, softened

2 cups flour

$^2/_3$ cup sugar

2 large eggs

2 teaspoons baking powder

1 teaspoon vanilla extract

$1^1/_2$ cups slivered almonds or finely chopped hazelnuts

Preheat the oven to 375°F. Lightly grease a cookie sheet.

Beat the butter in the bowl of a mixer until smooth. Add 1 cup of the flour, the sugar, eggs, baking powder, and vanilla, and mix. Stir in the remaining flour and the nuts.

Divide the dough in half. Shape each half into a 9-inch log that's about 2 inches thick. Place the logs about 4 inches apart on the cookie sheet, and bake them for 25 minutes. Allow the logs to cool on the sheet for 1 hour. Reduce the oven temperature to 325°F.

Cut each log on the diagonal into ½-inch slices. Place the slices cut side down on ungreased cookie sheets, and bake in 325°F oven for 8 to 10 minutes. Turn the slices over, and bake 8 to 10 minutes longer, until dry and crisp. Transfer the biscotti to a wire rack to cool.

new neighbor coffee

For some reason, breakfast just seems to be the most conducive meal for breaking the ice. Maybe it's because an invitation to breakfast is "low pressure" — you know it won't last too long, and the food will be familiar. Or maybe it's just because everyone loves to make what could be a lost moment of the day into something a little more ceremonial — and a whole lot more satisfying than a bagel on the run.

Every six months or so someone in my old Rye, New York, neighborhood hosts a morning coffee. Informal and friendly, these gatherings are a great way to catch up and to meet new neighbors. So working people can attend, it starts early and is very "open house." Usually a postcard is sent out a few weeks in advance, announcing when and where it will be held. The party lasts a few hours, and the host makes a point of walking about and introducing new neighbors to the established residents, pointing out who has kids of the same age or who shares interests and hobbies.

Neighborhood morning coffee ideas include the following:

- Until it's an established tradition, hosted by one heroic individual, make the gathering a potluck, asking a few people to bring a breakfast food — Danish, muffins, or fresh fruit. Or try co-hosting a morning coffee — it can spread the work and lets neighbors know it isn't just one person's idea of a party.

- Regular and decaf coffee should be on the menu, as well as milk and hot water with a selection of teas. Some hosts like to serve from china cups or mugs, but sturdy paper coffee cups are absolutely fine, too.

- If the group is going to be large, or if there are lots of new faces, make name tags. I know some people who really hate them, but unless a group is truly at home with one another, name tags make a big difference, helping to jog memories and get conversations started. Be sure to include each guest's street and house number, as well as his or her name.

- In general, babies should be welcome, but toddlers discouraged. A house full of toddlers means everyone, including moms, are distracted, and conversations tend to be interrupted.

- Depending on the reception your event gets, you may want to set a regular schedule for morning coffees, or simply schedule them as new residents arrive.

Getting new traditions to stick can be tricky. Sometimes one person keeps an event alive, while other events can rotate from home to home. A morning coffee is one that rotates well. Consider posting a sign-up sheet at the event asking for future hosts.

APRICOT NUT CAKE

makes 16 servings

My mom's good friend Dolly Smith first shared this rich cake with us, and it quickly became a household favorite. It keeps well.

- ¹/₄ pound plus 4 tablespoons (1¹/₂ sticks) butter
- 1¹/₂ cups sugar
- 3 large eggs
- ¹/₂ cup sour cream
- ¹/₄ teaspoon salt
- 1¹/₂ teaspoons baking powder
- 1¹/₂ teaspoons baking soda
- 3 cups sifted flour
- ¹/₂ cup chopped walnuts or pecans
- ¹/₂ cup sliced dried apricots
- 1 tablespoon ground cinnamon
- ¹/₄ cup sugar
- 3 tablespoons melted butter

Preheat the oven to 350°F.

In a large mixer bowl, cream the butter and 1¹/₂ cups sugar until pale and fluffy. Add the eggs one at a time; then add the sour cream.

Sift together the salt, baking powder, baking soda, and flour; then add the sifted ingredients to the butter mixture until well combined. Stir in the nuts and apricots.

Pour half the batter into a very well greased and floured Bundt pan. Sprinkle with half the cinnamon and then ¹/₈ cup of the sugar. Spoon the rest of the batter into the pan, and sprinkle again with the remaining cinnamon and sugar. Drizzle with the melted butter. Bake until the cake is golden brown and a cake tester inserted into the center comes out clean, about 1 hour. Cool the cake on a rack.

HILLS' BLUEBERRY CAKE

makes 6 to 8 servings

Betty Hills had a summerhouse in Gloucester, Massachusetts. Every summer the kids were sent to pick blueberries for this cake, which was eaten at breakfast, lunch, and dinner!

1½ cups flour

¾ cup sugar

3 tablespoons baking powder

3 tablespoons melted shortening

⅔ cup milk

1 large egg

¼ teaspoon salt

1 cup blueberries

Preheat the oven to 350°F. Grease a 9-inch round cake pan.

Mix the flour, sugar, and baking powder in a large bowl. Mix in the melted shortening, milk, egg, and salt, and blend until the mixture is smooth, about 2 minutes. Fold in the blueberries.

Pour the batter into the prepared pan, and bake until it's golden brown, about 30 minutes. Cool it on a rack. Serve this cake with a dollop of yogurt for breakfast or with ice cream for dessert.

RAISIN BREAD FRENCH TOAST

makes 10 to 12 servings

My friend Corrine discovered this wonderful breakfast and brunch dish when she stayed at Cyrus Kent House Inn in Chatham, Massachusetts. It's a perfect dish for potluck morning brunch.

1 (8-ounce) package cream cheese, softened

$^3/_4$ to 1 loaf sliced raisin bread

8 large eggs

$2^1/_2$ cups milk

$^1/_4$ cup maple syrup

6 tablespoons ($^3/_4$ stick) butter, melted

Lightly grease a 13 × 9–inch baking dish.

Spread the cream cheese on half the bread slices. Top these with the remaining slices. Cut the "sandwiches" into cubes, and place the cubes in the baking dish.

Mix the eggs, milk, maple syrup, and melted butter in a large bowl. Pour the egg mixture over the bread cubes. Press down on the mixture with a spatula to soak all the bread cubes. Cover the baking dish with foil, and refrigerate the cubes overnight.

Preheat the oven to 350°F.

Uncover the dish, and bake for 45 minutes, until the cubes are puffed and hot throughout. Cool the French toast for a few minutes; then divide into squares and serve.

2003 Back to School Buffet
Cia. raisin bread

FRUIT SALAD WITH HONEY FRENCH DRESSING

makes 12 servings

A touch of honey in the dressing brings out the sweetness of ripe fruits.

1 (20-ounce) can pineapple chunks in juice

1 cup melon balls (honeydew or cantaloupe)

3 bananas, sliced ½ inch thick

1 pint blueberries

1 pint strawberries, hulled and halved

dressing

³/₄ cup olive oil

¹/₄ cup vinegar

1 tablespoon toasted sesame seeds

1 tablespoon honey

¹/₂ teaspoon salt

¹/₄ teaspoon white pepper

¹/₄ teaspoon dry mustard

Drain the pineapple, reserving the juice. Dip the melon balls and banana slices in the juice, and combine in a bowl with the berries and pineapple.

Combine the pineapple juice with the oil, vinegar, sesame seeds, honey, salt, pepper, and mustard. Blend well.

Drizzle the salad with the dressing and serve.

VARIATION

Substitute ¼ teaspoon ground ginger for the sesame seeds.

the neighborhood directory

Any community can benefit from creating a neighborhood directory. It's something we've undertaken in every neighborhood I've lived in, and I'd be lost without one. A good directory contains such information as residents' nicknames, kids' names and ages, along with their phone numbers and street address. Instantly you know who is a potential baby-sitter, and knowing that it's Bob (not Rob) makes all the difference when you encounter the guy from across the street at the dry cleaner.

Get started by handing out a simple form for each family to fill out. Ask that it be returned by a specific date, or folks will procrastinate. (Even so, you'll have to pester the procrastinator—just plan on it.) Compile the information into a computer document that can be updated easily; then print and collate it. It's a nice touch to print the sheets horizontally and then fold them in half, like a mini phone book. You can add a card-stock cover with a piece of computer clip art on the front if you like, but it doesn't have to be fancy.

If your neighborhood has an existing list of phone numbers, why not update it now and add more information while you're at it?

Here are some things to include:

◆ E-mail addresses

◆ Pets and their names

◆ A list of kids who'd like to earn extra money by walking dogs, baby-sitting, shoveling snow, washing cars

◆ A bit of history about the neighborhood

◆ Trivia and oddments—who lived where, when

◆ Neighborhood events and their dates, or who's going to be in charge this year

Instead of folded pages, you might want to print a single sheet on both sides and have it laminated. At neighborhood events, have a sheet that anyone can pick up to update their listing for future editions, or for new neighbors to fill out.

a welcome cocktail party before you go

If you're selling your house, one of the most gracious things you can do for the new owners is to host a party for them. It can be as simple or elaborate as you want, but invite neighbors you know will make the new homeowner feel welcome. After the party, give the newcomers a list of those who attended—with a few notes to remind them who is who. By personally introducing them to your neighbors, you give everyone a head start on getting acquainted.

BUBBLIN' ARTICHOKE DIP

makes about 3 cups

Under the heading "oldies but goodies," you'll find this decadently rich cracker spread. Take care to buy artichoke hearts packed in water, not the marinated ones. Stir in some chopped cooked shrimp if you really want to go over the top.

1 (14-ounce) can artichoke hearts, drained and quartered

3/4 cup grated Parmesan cheese

1 cup mayonnaise

8 ounces shredded Monterey Jack cheese

Preheat the oven to 400°F. Grease a 1-quart casserole.

Combine the artichoke hearts, Parmesan cheese, and mayonnaise in a blender, and process until smooth. Pour the dip into the casserole. Sprinkle the shredded cheese over the top. Bake the dip at 400°F for 15 minutes.

STUFFED CUCUMBER WHEELS

makes 18 servings as an appetizer

Pink salmon and green olives rolled into cucumber wheels are colorful, flavorful, and fast to make. Make sure you use unwaxed cukes; look for them at the farmers' market or in the organic produce section of your market.

3 medium unwaxed cucumbers, scrubbed

1 (8-ounce) package cream cheese, softened

$1/2$ cup stuffed olives (or salad olives), finely chopped

$1/4$ cup chopped chives

2 ounces smoked salmon, chopped

Remove the ends from each cucumber, and halve the cucumbers lengthwise. Use a teaspoon to scoop the seeds from each half and discard them.

In a bowl, combine the cream cheese, olives, and chives, and blend well. Add the salmon, and blend until the stuffing is well mixed.

Stuff each cucumber half with the cheese mixture, reassemble the halves, and press them together.

Wrap the cucumbers in plastic wrap and refrigerate them for 12 to 24 hours. To serve, cut them into $1/4$-inch slices, and fan the wheels onto a serving tray.

COCKTAIL POTATO PANCAKES

Potato pancakes are the perfect pass-around canapé to serve when you want to make a good impression. Top these charmers with caviar, chopped black olives, smoked salmon, minced chives, or dill or another herb of your choice, depending on the occasion, the crowd, and your budget.

2 medium baking potatoes (russet or Yukon Gold), peeled

$1/2$ small onion

1 garlic clove minced ($1/2$ teaspoon), optional

1 large egg

1 tablespoon fresh marjoram (1 teaspoon dried)

$1/4$ teaspoon salt

Freshly ground black pepper

1 tablespoon all-purpose flour

$1/4$ teaspoon baking powder

$1/4$ cup peanut or corn oil

$1/2$ cup sour cream

In a food processor or by hand, grate the potatoes, onion, and garlic. Transfer to a sieve, and set aside to drain for 15 minutes or so.

In a medium bowl, combine the egg, marjoram, salt, and pepper, and beat until well blended. Add the potato mixture, flour, and baking powder.

In a large frying pan, warm 2 tablespoons of the oil over medium heat. Drop tablespoons of potato batter into the hot pan, and flatten them with the back of a spoon. Cook the pancakes, turning once, until golden brown on both sides, about 5 minutes in all. Drain them on paper towels. Repeat the process with the remaining batter, adding more oil to the pan as needed. (If you are making the pancakes in advance, cover and refrigerate them for up to 2 days. Before serving, arrange them in a single layer on a baking sheet, and bake at 450°F for about 5 minutes.)

Serve 2 pancakes on a small plate with a fork, garnished with 1 teaspoon sour cream and a dab of any topping you can think of.

New neighbors are new for a long time. If you don't get something over in the first few days or weeks after they arrive, it's okay. Getting attention only at the top of the move can be disheartening. Also, don't forget that new kids are often really lonely in their brand-new homes. Encourage your child to make an effort to include the new kids in outings and neighborhood games.

DEVILED CRAB

makes 4 cups, enough for
8 servings as an entrée,
24 as an appetizer

Serve deviled crab on a sideboard with a favorite cracker. Truly tasty!

6 tablespoons ($^3/_4$ stick) butter

$^1/_2$ cup chopped green bell pepper

$^1/_2$ cup chopped onion

$^1/_4$ cup chopped celery

1 tablespoon chopped fresh tarragon
(1 teaspoon dried)

1 tablespoon Worcestershire sauce

Dash of hot pepper sauce

1 teaspoon dry mustard

1 teaspoon salt

1 teaspoon freshly ground black pepper

$^1/_4$ cup plus 2 tablespoons flour

2 cups milk

2 pounds lump crabmeat, picked over

1 (2-ounce) jar drained minced pimiento

$^1/_2$ cup fine dry bread crumbs

Preheat the broiler. Butter a shallow ovenproof serving dish or gratiné pan.

Melt 4 tablespoons of the butter in a large skillet over medium heat. Add the green pepper, onion, celery, tarragon, Worcestershire, hot sauce, mustard, salt, and pepper. Cook, stirring occasionally, until the vegetables are softened but not browned.

Mix in the flour and cook, stirring, until the mixture is light golden. Gradually stir in the milk, mixing to get out any lumps. Bring to a boil and then cook, stirring often until the mixture thickens. Stir in the crab and pimiento.

Transfer the crab mixture to the prepared pan, sprinkle bread crumbs on top, and dot with the remaining 2 tablespoons of butter. Broil about 6 inches from heat until the crumbs are lightly browned and the mixture is bubbly, about 3 to 5 minutes.

SHRIMP DIP

makes 4 cups

This dip's good with crackers, bread, or crisp veggies. Keep it covered and cold until party time.

8 ounces cream cheese, softened

1 cup mayonnaise

3 tablespoons chili sauce or salsa

2 tablespoons fresh lemon or lime juice

1 small onion, grated

1 pound cooked bay shrimp or peeled medium shrimp, chopped

Combine the cream cheese, mayonnaise, chili sauce, lemon or lime juice, and onion. Blend well. Fold in the shrimp, and transfer the dip to a serving bowl. It may be kept refrigerated and covered for up to 2 days.

PROSCIUTTO-and-GRUYÈRE PINWHEELS

pinwheels

makes 12 servings as an appetizer

These appetizers are so good, and better still, you make the roll-up in advance. Slice the pinwheels when you want them, and bake. They also heat well in the microwave.

3/4 cup finely grated Gruyère (about 3 ounces)

4 teaspoons chopped fresh sage leaves

1 puff pastry sheet (from one 17 1/4-ounce package frozen puff pastry sheets), thawed

1 large egg, lightly beaten

2 ounces thinly sliced prosciutto

In a bowl, combine the Gruyère and sage. Arrange the pastry sheet on a lightly floured surface with a short side facing you. Cut the sheet in half crosswise.

Arrange 1/2 of the sheet with a long side facing you, and brush the edge of the far side with some egg. Arrange half the prosciutto evenly on top of the pastry, avoiding the egg-brushed edge, and top with half of the Gruyère mixture.

Starting with the side nearest you, roll the pastry jelly-roll fashion into a log, and wrap it in waxed paper. Make another log in the same manner. Wrap the logs tightly in plastic, and chill, seams down, until firm, for at least 3 hours and up to 3 days.

To serve, preheat the oven to 400°F. Lightly grease 2 large baking sheets. Remove the wrappings, and cut the logs crosswise into 1/2-inch-thick pinwheels. Arrange, cut sides down, 1 inch apart on baking sheets. Bake pinwheels in batches in the middle of the oven until golden, 14 to 16 minutes. Transfer the pinwheels to a rack, cool slightly, and serve warm.

CRABMEAT-AND-SHRIMP SURPRISE

makes 18 servings as an appetizer

Rich, rich, rich. For a dramatic presentation, serve this whole on the sideboard. Cut the first two slices . . . and let your neighbors do the rest.

1	pound cream cheese
1	small red onion
1½	pounds crabmeat or mock crabmeat (surimi)
1½	teaspoons paprika
½	teaspoon cayenne pepper
	Dash of white pepper
½	teaspoon salt
3	cups precooked shrimp (thawed frozen shrimp works fine)
1	frozen puff pastry sheet, thawed
1	egg yolk, lightly beaten with 1 tablespoon of water

Preheat the oven to 375°F.

Place the cheese, onion, crabmeat, all the spices, and the salt in a food processor. Pulse until it's blended but not creamed. Add the shrimp, and pulse a few more times.

Place the pastry sheet on a cookie sheet. Spread the crabmeat mixture to within about an inch of each edge. Fold the top of the sheet over the mixture, and bring the front up so that you can pinch a seam all the way across. Fold the ends up, as well, and pinch them tightly so that the entire mixture is in a sealed pouch. Score the top lightly by dragging a knife through just the very top layer of the pastry. Brush the entire parcel with the egg wash.

Bake for 30 to 40 minutes, until well browned. Let stand for 15 minutes before slicing into 2-inch pieces.

the very busy, there-is-no-time-to-meet ladies' lunch

Who in her right mind would introduce another social event in that hectic time right before the holidays? Kay Langan in Greenwich, Connecticut, did just that when she came up with this idea that is now in its sixteenth year and run by a committee of women. A practical, action-oriented woman and a terrific entertainer, Kay wanted to organize a luncheon for the very busy women in her area because everyone she spoke to seemed so loaded down with to-do lists that they never had any time to stay in touch with old neighbors — or meet new ones.

So she decided to make time and invited the world. Kay lived on a peninsula of land cut off from the rest of town by an interstate highway. She didn't let the fact that she didn't know all three hundred families in the area deter her; she went to the town hall, got the land records for her area, and used it to develop her invite list. Accordingly, three hundred women got an invitation to "The Busy Ladies' Lunch."

Kay wanted to make her invitation hard to decline, so she made the event as loose as possible. Her invitation read, "Everybody's busy, but you gotta eat sometime. Come in a suit, come in tennis shorts, just come." To ensure that women with different types of commitments would be able to squeeze in a visit, she scheduled it from 11:00 A.M. to 3:30 P.M.

The menu was easy and smart. Here's how she set up her party:

- She made vast quantities of a fabulous homemade soup and bought small muffins to accompany it.

- Her entire dining room table was set up as a make-your-own salad bar with tossed greens, all the fixings, and a choice of salad dressings, plus oil and vinegar cruets. Each dressing was identified with a place-card holder. It was an easy menu that worked perfectly for a party that lasted a relatively long time.

- Kay used paper plates, and sturdy, disposable paper mugs for the soup. Beverages included white wine, some sodas, and bottled water.

- Coffee and trays of homemade cookies and brownies followed.

- She provided blank name tags and insisted that each guest wear one.

THE BUSY LADIES' LUNCH SOUP

makes 6 to 10 servings

This recipe doubles or triples easily. To serve a hundred ladies, you'll need to make multiple batches. Serve as a first course in teacup-size portions. In the summer, stir half a cup of nonfat plain yogurt into each batch, and serve cold.

2 tablespoons butter

1 yellow onion, coarsely chopped

$^1/_2$ pound carrots, coarsely chopped

1 teaspoon curry powder

1 (20-ounce) can plum tomatoes, coarsely chopped, with juice

$3^1/_2$ cups chicken broth

2 tablespoons dried basil

Salt and pepper to taste

Melt the butter in a soup pot. Add the onion, and cook over medium heat for 5 minutes. Add the carrots and curry powder, cover, and cook over medium heat for 20 minutes, until the vegetables are tender. Add the tomatoes and chicken broth. Bring the soup to a boil, lower the heat, and simmer for 20 minutes. Add the basil and the salt and pepper, and simmer for 2 more minutes.

Working in batches, blend in a food processor or blender until smooth. (A handheld wand blender is especially good for this.)

AMERICAN BLUE CHEESE DRESSING

makes about 1 cup

We like this best made with Maytag Blue Cheese from Iowa.

1 large garlic clove

1 teaspoon kosher salt

1 teaspoon dry mustard

1 tablespoon fresh lemon juice

1 tablespoon balsamic vinegar

2 tablespoons light olive oil

2/3 cup sour cream

2 tablespoons mayonnaise

2 scallions, finely chopped

3 ounces American blue cheese

Freshly ground black pepper to taste

Place the garlic and salt on a cutting board, or in a mortar and pestle, and chop or mash until they form a paste. Transfer the garlic paste to a bowl, and work in the mustard powder. Whisk in the lemon juice and vinegar. Slowly whisk in the oil.

In another bowl, combine the sour cream and mayonnaise, and slowly whisk this mixture into the garlic mixture. Stir in the scallions and blue cheese. Season with the pepper, and serve.

CREAMY YOGURT-MUSTARD DRESSING

makes 2 cups

A tart, smooth dressing that is a low-fat alternative to vinaigrettes.

Juice of 2 lemons
1/4 cup extra virgin olive oil
3 tablespoons Dijon mustard
2 teaspoons salt
1 teaspoon freshly ground black pepper
3 garlic cloves, roughly chopped
2 cups plain low-fat yogurt

Combine the lemon juice, olive oil, mustard, salt, pepper, and garlic in a blender, and puree until smooth. Add the yogurt, and blend briefly to combine.

HERB GARLIC CROUTONS

herb garlic croutons

makes 3 cups

Of course these are great in a salad, but try floating a handful of them in a mug of steaming soup. Pack some of these fragrant flavor-boosters in a colorful tin along with a pot of soup for a heartwarming, glad-to-know-ya gift.

2 tablespoons unsalted butter

3 tablespoons extra virgin olive oil

3 cups stale $^1/_2$-inch bread cubes

2 large garlic cloves, minced ($1^1/_2$ teaspoons)

1 teaspoon chopped fresh parsley

1 teaspoon snipped fresh chives

1 teaspoon chopped fresh tarragon

3 tablespoons freshly grated Parmesan cheese

Heat the butter and oil in a large nonstick skillet. Add the bread cubes and cook them over medium-high heat, tossing them constantly with a wooden spoon, for 3 to 4 minutes. Reduce the heat to medium-low.

Add the garlic and herbs to the bread cubes. Continue to cook the croutons, tossing them frequently, until they are golden brown, about 20 minutes. Transfer them to a bowl, and toss with the Parmesan. Cool the croutons to room temperature, and store them in an airtight container until you're ready to use them.

the what's where list

Here's a gift that fits every new neighbor, because there's nothing in the world that's more helpful when you're new to a community and have to start the tedious process of locating a good dry cleaner or dentist. I have been given a list each time I've moved into a new neighborhood, and it is always invaluable. Now I add my own discoveries and annotations to the list and pass it along to new arrivals.

A What's Where List outlines all the resources you have come to rely on in your community, the kind of stuff that you and your neighbors figured out over years of trial and error—and that you wish you'd known on Day One. No one's obligated to use your suggestions, but at the very least it gives a person a starting point.

Here are some things to include:

- Dry cleaner/seamstress/tailor
- Pediatrician
- Lawn and tree care service
- Dentist
- OB/GYN
- Biggest, best-stocked grocery store
- Farmers' market
- Gourmet shop
- Housekeeping or cleaning service
- Favorite restaurants
- Nearby takeout locations
- Locksmith

- Painter
- Plumber
- Electrician
- Roofer
- Veterinarian
- Handyman/carpenter
- After-school programs
- Baby-sitters

Make the list more specific if you see your new neighbor is into gardening or jogs regularly, or has other hobbies. You might suggest great nurseries or give information on fun jogging trails and local 10K races. Be sure to update this list regularly and add your phone number, as well, in case the recipient has any questions.

the block party

Neighborhood block parties involve all the residents of a designated area. They can include contests, talent shows, games for adults, games for kids, goofy races, and sing-alongs, and a meal is always part of the proceedings. Some block parties are annual events and loaded with traditions, but thousands of new block parties start up each year.

The Grill Station

Perfectly Spicy Grilled Chicken 53

The Only Way Bratwurst 54

Herb's Mustard 55

Zesty Blue Cheese Topping 56

Green Tomato Chutney Topping 57

Grilled Quesadillas 58

Sides and Salads

Baked Beans 59

Noodles with Creamy Peanut Sauce 60

Broccoli-and-Raisin Salad 61

Orzo Salad with Feta, Olives, and Bell Peppers 62

Taffy Apple Salad 63

Italian Pasta Salad 64

Italian Vinaigrette 65

Picnic Potato Salad 67

Beefy Guacamole Soft Tacos 68

Layered Bean Dip 69

Desserts

Peanut Butter and Chocolate Crispie Squares 72

Liza's Lemon Squares 73

Marble Blondies 74

Mom's Brownies 75

Coffee Ice Cream Cake 76

Ranger Cookies 77

Creating ways for the whole neighborhood to gather can be the most fun of all. They're a chance to catch up, share stories, and solidify the notion that despite our hectic lives and diverse interests, we share a living space and therefore are connected to one another. Make no mistake: a block party is a big undertaking that requires significant planning, organization, and energy. This chapter will tell you everything you need to know to establish a treasured neighborhood tradition or improve upon an existing one. I'll cover exactly what you need to get started, offer recipes that are easy to make and feed a crowd, and suggest some fun ways to make your block party memorable.

Some general words of caution and common sense are in order. Not everyone loves to plan neighborhood events. Not everyone has time to help. Not everyone

who says they'll come will show up or bring the dish they said they would. That's okay. All of us have months or years in which there is simply too much going on in our lives to focus on the neighborhood. Don't take it personally, and try to remember that next year it might be *you* with too much on your plate! Keep it light, keep it inclusive, and assure folks they'll be welcome next year. Recognize, too, that there are lots of ways to help, and they are *all* good. Some people love to organize, and some don't want the responsibility. Some want to be told what to bring, and others have their hearts set on a particular dish they want to contribute. Accept any and all assistance with a smile, and you will never lack for volunteers.

the food

In every group there are always a few generous souls who love to cook for a crowd and can be counted on to provide fabulous dishes. Chances are, though, you'll need to augment their contributions with foods that are purchased or cooked on-site. Consider how many people are invited, the number of kids expected, and if it's your first block party, how reliable people will be. For whatever reason, some people will offer to bring a salad and then simply forget. Make it clear that those who are short on time are welcome to bring something store-bought — deli salads and desserts are good candidates.

The safest approach is to have some food supplied and some food brought

potluck style. If you don't ask people to bring any food at all, you eliminate part of the shared experience of the block party. Many people love to bring their favorite salads, sides, and desserts. Those who don't cook should be encouraged to sign up for other chores.

One route many groups take is to set up several long tables where potluck contributions can be deposited: one for condiments, one for salads and side dishes, one for desserts. (Set up yet another table for beverages, in a different area.) The more variety you can feature on the sides-and-salad table, the better. This is a terrific place for folks to show off their cultural heritage with traditional ethnic or family dishes.

Recipes for especially well-received dishes might even be printed in your neighborhood newsletter, although you should avoid the temptation to make this a competitive event.

A grilling station is the centerpiece of many block party menus, and with good reason. Grilling makes the party lively and involving, and it gives people who may not know each other very well something to talk about. Certainly you could order a six-foot hero sandwich as the main meal for your block party, but grilling burgers and dogs is more communal and probably tastes better, too.

If you do grill, you'll need one gas or charcoal grill for every forty people in attendance. If you're expecting a really large crowd of over a hundred people, renting oversize grills, which can serve hundreds of people, might make more sense. These can be set up and picked up by the rental outfit, and they're easy to use and relatively cheap.

To get a handle on how much food to prepare, review your RSVPs. As a general rule, some may eat two hot dogs or hamburgers, but some will only eat the side dishes—still, plan extra. Most small kids prefer hot dogs to hamburgers, so make sure you've got plenty of dogs.

Buying hamburgers and hot dogs in large quantities is the simplest way to get started, but you may want to have more variety coming off the grill. Homemade condiments will also make the meal a little special. And a simple grilled appetizer might also be just right for your crowd. The recipes that follow offer plenty of ideas for grilled entrées and appetizers, plus a great variety of salads, condiments, and drinks to round out the menu. Each one has been to dozens of block parties and is always invited back year after year!

planning your block party

The neighborhood events that seem to work best have a winning combination of creative thinking and solid organization. If you are spearheading this year's effort, here are some things to remember:

Get Help. Don't try to plan a block party alone. (Why would anyone want that hassle, anyway?) Form a committee to spread the workload and to make certain everyone knows that it's not just one person's idea of a party—it's a group endeavor. (Be sure your invitation or posters indicate it's a group effort, too.)

Be Inclusive. If your area is a mix of young families and older people, recruit help that reflects this mix. That will help to ensure that everyone who should be invited is. The more people you involve, the greater the sense of ownership and the more creative the party can be. Place a few calls to float the possibility of a block party. Solicit not only ideas but also names of people who might help.

Listen. The most important qualification for anyone putting the event together is a good ear. You must be willing to hear suggestions and look for ways to incorporate them into the plans.

shopping and money

If you are going to be collecting donations, you want the request to be reasonable and the money to be spent efficiently. Decide if the donation will be individual, per family, per adult, per child. Whatever you decide needs to be fair and easy. Many block parties ask for a family donation. The amount will depend on what you're serving, if there is alcohol, and if the fee is contributing to any of the activities or rentals. Try to keep it reasonable. A block party of thirty families at ten bucks per family gets you three hundred dollars. If that just needs to cover food and drink, you're in good shape. Should there be any money left over, make sure it is applied to next year's party and that you adjust the donation accordingly.

If you live near one of those warehouse clubs—and who doesn't these days—one big shopping trip can cover nearly all the basics and save you a lot of money. Buying in bulk may leave you with plenty of leftover paper goods, but you can box them up and use them next year.

Here's a very basic list to take with you to the store:

- Preshaped hamburgers. Get high-quality ones; there isn't much price difference, but there is a big taste difference.
- Hot dogs
- Bratwurst
- Buns
- Ketchup
- Mustard and mayonnaise
- Lettuce, tomatoes, sliced onions
- Relish
- Pickles
- Very sturdy paper plates
- Napkins
- Forks
- 12-ounce paper cups
- Paper tablecloths

Hang on to your receipts for any shopping. Not only do you want to be able to tally your expenses, but after the party you'll also want to compare how much you bought with what was left over so that you can adjust next year's shopping list.

who gets invited?

In some areas it is obvious which houses, apartments, or streets constitute the neighborhood. If you live on a cul-de-sac, that may be your boundary. A river, a highway, or a busy street may define your area. What is most important is that you think through the area that is included ahead of time. Nothing spoils a generous effort to bring people together faster than discovering you neglected to include someone. If you live in an area with alleys, do you want to involve the families who live in the homes across the way?

One neighborhood I know of deliberately invited the residents of a new apartment complex that went up behind them, because they wanted to make sure those people knew the history of the area and would feel more invested in keeping it clean and safe. Another group decided to throw a block party that included more than twenty-three blocks and three hundred families. It was a massive and complicated affair, but it worked.

If you have any doubts about where to draw the line, talk it over. It's okay to start small and stay small. You may decide after the first year that the party could have been bigger and you grow the list for year two. The bottom line is that you need reasons for your decisions that are logical and not arbitrary.

Once you determine the area, it is essential that you invite every single family, person, and member of that area. It's not a neighborhood block party if you don't. Even if you're convinced certain people wouldn't be interested, you must give them the chance to say no. And don't be surprised if they say yes!

invitations

There are lots of ways to let neighbors know about a block party. Your area may lend itself to posters, but many busy folks appreciate getting something they can tape to the refrigerator or hold while they mark it in their calendar. If this is the first block party, consider sending the invitation out in two parts, one several weeks after the other.

The first invitation should go out early, eight to ten weeks before the party itself. It should specify the date, time, and location if possible, and it should include your name and at least one, if not more, name of people who are organizing it. Include an RSVP phone number, as well. By sending it out far enough in advance, people will have time to ask questions, raise concerns, contribute, and most important, buy into the idea of a block party. Remember, you need to be willing to handle issues that come up and welcome new suggestions.

Make clear in this invitation that food will be served and indicate that a small fee will be collected to cover some of the expenses if that is the case. You should also make it clear if alcohol will be served. If you are planning a talent show or a contest, that, too, should be in the first invitation, in a tone that welcomes participation. This first invitation is also an opportunity to solicit volunteers and let people know what you'll need. Keep the list short and clear, but specify if you'll need any of the following:

- Folding tables, ice chests, coolers, chairs, or grills
- Someone to organize and man the grills
- Someone to be responsible for beverages
- Someone to organize kids' activities
- An individual to be in charge of the RSVPs and head count

When you draft your first invitation, spend a few minutes designing a layout that is memorable, and plan on using the same layout and the same paper for the follow-up invitation. People get bombarded with mail, and you don't want yours lost in the shuffle. Printing the invitation on card stock makes it easier to keep track of.

If you are delivering the invitations to each home, you should be aware that technically it is illegal to put anything into another person's mailbox. Taping the invite to the door or slipping it underneath are good alternatives, but whatever you decide, make the effort to ensure that your invitation actually gets to the recipient. If you rely on a neighborhood kid to pass out the invitations, choose one who is highly reliable. I know a neighbor who did not find her invitation until after the fact. The child had put it in a place she didn't think to look. Even though she'd heard an event was planned, she was too embarrassed to say anything when she didn't receive an invite, and so she didn't go.

The second invitation should go out three weeks before the block party, on the same stock as the first. It should firm up specific party elements, such as potluck instructions, talent show, and donation amount. The date and start time should be big and bold.

timing

Schedule your block party for a date when the greatest number of people in the neighborhood will be able to come, and when it's warm enough to take place outside. That rules out the middle of summer, when people may be on vacation, and, for much of the country, the winter months. If you are just getting started, I would also steer clear of holidays like Labor Day and Fourth of July because many people will already have other plans.

Choose a weekend when school is in session so that you have a good shot at getting all the families with kids. Some neighborhoods throw their block parties in early to mid June and some aim for September, after Labor Day. Don't forget to look at a calendar to be certain you have considered any religious holidays that might conflict, as well as townwide events, such as a major charity run or festival.

Many block parties take place on Sunday afternoons. Saturdays are often filled with other obligations, and having the event on Sunday gives volunteers a day to do shopping or setting up.

getting organized

You can make your block party as elaborate as your time and imagination allow. It all comes down to how creative your group is, how hard you want to work, and how organized you all can be. There are four basic areas you need to plan: the setup, the food, the activities, and the cleanup. If it's your first year, consider keeping it relatively simple. It is always easier to build on a solid foundation than try to explain, "We'll get it right next year." Keep a record of what you do that first year, from how many hamburgers you bought, to who volunteered for what. Those records will be extremely useful next year.

One of the things that makes a block party fun is that much of it takes place in the street. There's something exciting and special about having kids and adults wandering around on what is usually car turf, and the venue reinforces the fact that this party belongs to everyone.

Start by putting in a call to the local police to determine if a permit is necessary to close off the street. If it's not possible to close off the entire street, ask if at least one lane can be shut down. Don't be discouraged if you cannot have your party in the street, though; you want your party as close to the neighborhood as possible, but if it can't be physically in the neighborhood, you can still have a wonderful event nearby. Consider any alleys, school playgrounds, public squares, or parks in the area. Regardless of where the party is held, you must nail down the location before the second invitation goes out.

If your block party is going to be very big, you should alert the fire department and ask if there are any local ordinances that you'll need to follow. Make sure to send a letter confirming your request a week before the event.

Next, think through how the party should be laid out. Keep in mind that the grilling should be done away from any activities with small children. If you have an elderly population attending, you'll want to have a place for them to sit while eating, preferably at a table. If there is a pool in the neighborhood that will be open to kids during the event, make certain there will be adult supervision at all times.

How spread out do you want the party? Some block parties have games going on in one place, food in another, and so forth. Lay out on paper where all the activities will take place. If it is going to be a very large party, make sure the layout doesn't have any bottlenecks. For instance, don't put beer right next to the hors d'oeuvre table. Spread things out a bit so people will have a reason to move about.

Here are some other things to consider:

- Do you need power? Some games may require electricity, and if there is a band, they'll need to plug in their equipment.
- Do you need running water?
- How far are you dragging the grills?
- Do you want a separate area for appetizers?
- Do you want a game area for older kids that's separate from the toddlers' activities?
- Do you need any kind of a stage?
- How many folding tables will you need? Will you be able to borrow enough of them, or should you rent?
- Do you want guests to be able to sit while they eat? Some parties are BYOC (bring your own chair). Some aren't, and people mingle and enjoy their meal standing. Your invitation might read, "If you want a chair to sit on, please bring it."
- Should you provide any shade?
- Who will serve as cleanup crew?

PERFECTLY SPICY GRILLED CHICKEN

I've prepared this chicken a zillion times, and it's a guaranteed winner. A single chicken breast fillet works well on a bun, but you can also cut the chicken into strips and grill them for a great appetizer.

8 garlic cloves, smashed

1/2 cup chopped fresh ginger

1/2 cup soy sauce

1 cup fresh lemon juice

4 teaspoons hot red pepper sauce

1/4 cup red wine vinegar

1 cup extra virgin olive oil

1 teaspoon ground black pepper

16 boneless, skinless chicken breast fillets

In a large sealable plastic bag, combine all the ingredients except the chicken. Seal the bag and shake. Place the chicken in the bag with the marinade, and refrigerate it for at least 1 hour. (If all the chicken doesn't fit, divide the marinade between 2 bags.) Turn the bag over at least twice to make certain the marinade reaches all the pieces.

Place the chicken on a hot grill, and cook on each side about 7 minutes, or until the breasts are cooked through.

THE ONLY WAY BRATWURST

makes 8 to 10 servings

If you're ready to move beyond simple wieners, go all out with the brats. Parboiling them in a beer bath makes them extra good.

2 pounds bratwurst

2 onions, thinly sliced

$\frac{1}{2}$ pound (2 sticks) butter or margarine

6 (12-ounce) cans beer

$1\frac{1}{2}$ teaspoons ground black pepper

Prick the bratwursts all over with a fork so they won't explode as they cook. Place in a large pot with the onions and butter, and slowly pour in the beer. Bring to a boil over medium heat; then reduce the heat and simmer for 15 to 20 minutes.

Preheat the grill. Lightly oil the grate, and place the bratwursts on the grill. Cook the bratwursts for 10 to 14 minutes over medium-hot coals, turning them to brown evenly. Serve these hot off the grill.

HERB'S MUSTARD

makes 1 cup

Spread on a hot toasted hamburger bun and enjoy!

2 tablespoons fresh tarragon (2 teaspoons dried)

$^1/_4$ cup minced parsley

1 tablespoon lemon juice

4 heaping teaspoons Dijon mustard

4 tablespoons ($^1/_2$ stick) butter, halved lengthwise

Combine the tarragon and parsley in a bowl, and stir in the lemon juice and mustard. Place the butter on top, cover the bowl with plastic wrap, and set it aside for 30 to 40 minutes, until the butter softens.

Blend the butter into the herb mixture with a fork. Transfer the mustard to a small bowl. Cover the bowl, and keep it refrigerated until you're ready to use it.

Rain Date

Some groups like to designate a rain date. I think that's a tough call because turnout for a rescheduled event is inevitably much lighter, and the endless phone calls and confusion that arise from the "Will we or won't we?" can be a real downer. Depending on where you live, rain can be a real threat or a remote possibility. I generally don't plan a rain date, and would keep the party on even if rain is forecast. Rarely does it rain for hours, and a light drizzle in warm weather isn't the worst thing. If it does rain in earnest, you may be able to serve food from a handy garage on the block or someone's covered porch.

ZESTY BLUE CHEESE TOPPING

makes 1 cup

This will wake up an ordinary burger.

1 large garlic clove

4 ounces blue cheese, crumbled

4 ounces cream cheese, cut into 6 pieces

10 drops red hot pepper sauce

$^2/_3$ cup vegetable oil

In the bowl of a food processor and with the machine running, drop the garlic through the feed tube to mince it. Add the cheeses and pepper sauce. Process until the mixture is smooth, about 45 seconds, scraping down the bowl as necessary. With the machine running, add the oil in a steady stream. Transfer this topping to a bowl, cover it, and refrigerate it until serving time.

Set up a sign-in table with:

- Name tags and pens — they are must-haves
- News about upcoming events or solicitation for ideas
- A neighborhood directory sign-up sheet. A block party is a great opportunity to get nicknames and ages of kids and pets, correct addresses, and whatever else makes sense for sharing with the whole block.

GREEN TOMATO CHUTNEY TOPPING

Use the last of your backyard tomatoes to make this tangy condiment for hamburgers, chicken, or brats.

2 pounds green tomatoes, cored and sliced

1 pound tart green apples, peeled, cored, and sliced

²/₃ cup water

³/₄ cup sugar

2 tablespoons white vinegar

¹/₂ teaspoon salt

¹/₂ teaspoon ground cinnamon

¹/₄ to ¹/₂ teaspoon ground cloves

¹/₂ teaspoon ground ginger

Preheat the oven to 375°F.

Combine the tomatoes, apples, and water in a large roasting pan. Cover the pan tightly with foil, and bake (stirring after 30 minutes) until the apples and tomatoes are soft, about 1 hour. Remove the pan from the oven, but leave the oven on.

Transfer the baked mixture to a food processor, and pulse it on and off for about 4 seconds, until the topping is chunky; return it to the pan, and stir in the remaining ingredients.

Bake, uncovered, until the topping is thickened, about 1 hour. If a crust begins to form, stir the mixture. Cool the chutney completely before transferring it to tightly sealed glass jars. You may refrigerate the chutney for up to 2 weeks.

GRILLED QUESADILLAS

Here's a simple but delicious appetizer to make during a block party. It's just the kind of icebreaker a first-time party could use. Use a bag of preshredded Mexican mixed cheese to cut down the prep time.

12 (6-inch) flour tortillas

1 (16-ounce) can refried beans

8 ounces shredded Cheddar, mozzarella, or Monterey Jack cheese

1 cup guacamole (store-bought is fine)

1 (3-ounce) can chopped green chiles, drained well

2 tablespoons extra virgin olive oil

Spread 6 of the tortillas with refried beans. Sprinkle them with cheese, and top with a dollop of guacamole and a few chiles. Cover each with a second tortilla.

Brush the grill with the olive oil. Place the tortillas on the rack, and grill them until the bottoms are slightly browned. Flip the quesadillas carefully with a large spatula, and cook them until the other side is toasted.

Transfer the quesadillas to a cutting board. Let them cool for a few minutes; then cut each one into 6 or 8 wedges with a pizza cutter. Serve these appetizers while they're hot.

BAKED BEANS

What summer picnic is complete without baked beans? And who knew they were so easy to make from scratch? You'll feel just like a pioneer, and the kids will love you.

1 pound dried navy or great northern beans, sorted and rinsed

$1/2$ cup brown sugar

3 tablespoons dark molasses

$1/2$ teaspoon baking soda

$1/2$ teaspoon dry mustard

1 teaspoon salt

$1/2$ -pound piece salt pork, optional

In a large saucepan, combine the beans with enough water to cover them by 2 inches. Bring to a boil; then reduce the heat and simmer for 20 minutes. Drain the beans.

Preheat the oven to 350°F.

In a heavy casserole with a lid, mix together the beans, brown sugar, molasses, baking soda, mustard, and salt. Add the salt pork. Cover the casserole and bake for about 4½ hours. Check the beans frequently while they're baking, and add water as needed to maintain a thick, soupy consistency, stirring occasionally.

NOODLES WITH CREAMY PEANUT SAUCE

Even picky eaters seem to love the mildly exotic flavors of this Thai-inspired dish. Adding shredded cooked chicken or shrimp makes it a one-dish meal.

10 ounces thin Chinese egg noodles or spaghettini

$1/2$ cup smooth peanut butter

$1/3$ cup chicken stock

$1/4$ cup soy sauce

$1/4$ cup Asian sesame oil (available at Asian markets)

2 tablespoons minced garlic (12 cloves)

2 tablespoons minced ginger

2 tablespoons sugar

2 tablespoons red wine vinegar

2 teaspoons hot pepper oil (available at Asian markets) or Tabasco sauce

$1/4$ cup milk

In a large pot, bring 3 quarts of water to a boil. Add the noodles, and cook them until they are just al dente. Drain the noodles in a colander, rinse them under running cold water, and drain again well.

In a food processor fitted with the metal blade, or in a blender, blend all the remaining ingredients. Toss the noodles with the peanut sauce, and serve this dish warm or at room temperature.

BROCCOLI-AND-RAISIN SALAD

Nancy Dyer knows that if this is on the menu and I'm at her party, she had better double it. This salad should be made early, and tossed frequently before it is served.

6 cups of broccoli florets, cut into bite-size pieces

10 slices bacon, cooked and crumbled

$^2/_3$ cup raisins

$^1/_2$ red onion, finely chopped

2 cups shredded Cheddar cheese

1 to $1^1/_2$ cups mayonnaise

$^1/_4$ to $^1/_2$ cup sugar

2 to 3 tablespoons vinegar

Bring 2 cups of water to a boil in a large pot with a steamer insert. Steam the broccoli until it's tender-crisp, about 5 minutes. Drain.

In a large bowl, combine the broccoli, bacon, raisins, onion, and Cheddar.

Put the mayonnaise, sugar, and vinegar in another bowl, and mix them well. Pour ¾ cup of the dressing over the broccoli mixture, and mix well. Cover and refrigerate this salad for at least 2 hours and up to 6 hours before serving, tossing every hour or so. If the salad seems too dry, stir in the remaining dressing.

ORZO SALAD WITH FETA, OLIVES, AND BELL PEPPERS

makes 9 cups

With the addition of chopped roasted chicken this salad can be a hearty lunch.
If you can find it, try seasoned feta cheese; I like the basil-tomato flavor.

12 ounces orzo (rice-shaped pasta)

2 tablespoons plus $1/2$ cup extra virgin olive oil

$1^1/_2$ cups crumbled feta cheese, about 6 ounces

1 large red bell pepper, chopped (about 1 cup)

1 large yellow bell pepper, chopped (about 1 cup)

$^3/_4$ cup pitted Kalamata or other black olives

4 green onions, chopped

2 tablespoons drained capers

3 tablespoons fresh lemon juice

1 tablespoon white wine vinegar

1 tablespoon minced garlic (6 cloves)

$1^1/_2$ teaspoons dried oregano

1 teaspoon Dijon mustard

1 teaspoon ground cumin

Salt and pepper

3 tablespoons pine nuts, toasted in a 350°F oven for 7 minutes, or until golden

Bring a large pot of salted water to a boil. Cook the orzo until it's tender but still firm to the bite, about 12 minutes. Drain the pasta, rinse it with cold water, and drain it well. Transfer the orzo to large bowl, and toss it with the 2 tablespoons of olive oil.

Add the crumbled feta cheese, chopped bell peppers, Kalamata olives, green onions, and capers to the orzo, and mix them well.

Combine the lemon juice, vinegar, garlic, oregano, mustard, and cumin in a small bowl. Gradually whisk in the remaining ½ cup olive oil. Season this dressing to taste with salt and pepper.

Add the dressing to the orzo mixture, and toss it to blend. Season the salad to taste with salt and pepper. (The orzo salad can be prepared up to 6 hours ahead of time. Cover and refrigerate the salad.) Garnish with pine nuts, and serve.

TAFFY APPLE SALAD

makes 8 servings

This is a nice sweet fruit salad—perfect for a hot afternoon. Do I really need to add that it will be a particular hit with the younger party-goers?

- ½ cup sugar
- 1 tablespoon flour
- 2 tablespoons cider or white wine vinegar
- 1 (8-ounce) can crushed pineapple, with juice drained and reserved
- 1 large egg, well beaten
- 4 cups unpeeled, coarsely chopped apples
- 2 cups salted peanuts
- 8 ounces frozen nondairy topping

Combine the sugar, flour, vinegar, reserved pineapple juice, and the egg in a heavy saucepan. Mix the ingredients well and cook them over medium heat until the mixture thickens. Allow it to cool slightly.

Place the apples, peanuts, and drained pineapple in a bowl, and mix in the dressing. When the salad is completely cool, mix in the nondairy topping. Chill this salad for 1 hour before serving it.

ITALIAN PASTA SALAD

makes 8 to 12 servings as a side dish,
6 as an entrée

The key to making this salad especially pretty is cutting all the vegetables the same size. If you prefer, get out the food processor for a shortcut to one of my favorite salads. This recipe doubles and triples beautifully, and it always goes fast.

3 ounces sliced pepperoni

1 medium (6-ounce) zucchini, unpeeled

1/2 medium red onion

1/2 large (7-ounce) red bell pepper

1/2 large (7-ounce) green bell pepper

1 medium tomato

8 ounces cooked pasta, such as rotelli or penne

8 ounces cooked spinach pasta, such as rotelli or penne

12 to 14 jumbo pitted black olives, sliced

1/2 cup Italian Vinaigrette (see opposite page)

1/2 cup loosely packed Italian parsley, chopped

2 ounces shredded provolone cheese

Cut the pepperoni slices into matchstick strips and place in a 4-quart serving bowl. Cut the zucchini, onion, and red and green peppers into thin matchsticks and add to the bowl with the pepperoni. Slice the tomato into thin strips dice and add to the bowl, discarding the juice and seeds.

Add the pasta and olives to the meat-and-vegetable mixture and mix, then add the dressing and parsley, and toss well. Sprinkle the salad with the cheese, and serve at room temperature.

ITALIAN VINAIGRETTE

makes ¹/₂ cup

1 large garlic clove

¹/₂ cup extra virgin olive oil

2 tablespoons balsamic vinegar

2 tablespoons fresh basil leaves, cut into fine strips
(1 teaspoon dried)

¹/₂ teaspoon salt

¹/₄ teaspoon dried oregano

Freshly ground pepper

Drop the garlic clove into the feed tube of a running food processor, and chop until it is minced. Add the remaining ingredients, and process for 2 seconds.

block party beverages

Soda and water should be provided. Decide if you want individual cans of soda or large bottles. The downside of soda cans is that often a thirsty kid will open one, take two sips of it, and leave; then the child returns for another ten minutes later. You may find the cooler empty and dozens of nearly full cans on every table before you know it. I think it works best if you can set up a table or two with large plastic bottles, paper cups, and ice. Assign an adult to help pour for the very young ones. Jugs of lemonade and iced teas are good additions, too.

Many block parties also offer beer and wine for the adults. As a general rule, allow two beers per adult or one bottle of wine for every three adults. BYOB works well, too. You can also order a keg, which has the advantage of not creating empty bottles or cans to recycle.

You need ice to keep beer and soda cans cold, and you need ice to put in cups. Don't mix them. If you need more than one hundred pounds of ice, it may be more cost effective and time saving to order it in advance and have it delivered by an icehouse. Check your yellow pages for vendors.

One beverage you can probably skip is coffee. The old theory that you had to serve coffee at the end of a party to make sure any heavy drinker has a chance to sober up before driving doesn't apply to a block party, since the guests can just walk home. Coffee urns require electricity, as well as creamer, stirrers, special cups, and so forth. My advice—don't provide coffee unless it's the beverage of choice in your neighborhood.

PICNIC POTATO SALAD

potato salad

makes 20 servings

You can't call it a block party unless you serve potato salad. This version is
a classic.

4 pounds russet potatoes, peeled

1/2 cup white wine vinegar

1/2 cup extra virgin olive oil

1 teaspoon salt

1/4 teaspoon freshly ground black pepper

1 cup thinly sliced red onions

1 cup celery strips, 1/4 inch

3 medium cucumbers, peeled, seeded, and sliced

2 cups mayonnaise (and more if needed)

5 tablespoons prepared Dijon or herb mustard

20 hard-boiled eggs, peeled and quartered

1 cup chopped Italian parsley

Drop the potatoes into a large pot of cold salted water as you peel
them. Bring the water to a boil, and cook until the potatoes are tender but still firm, 20 to 30 minutes.

Drain the potatoes, and roughly slice them into a very large mixing
bowl. Sprinkle the still-hot potatoes with vinegar, olive oil, salt, and
pepper, and toss gently.

Add the onions, celery, cucumbers, mayonnaise, and mustard, and
toss gently to combine. Add the quartered eggs and parsley, and toss
again. Cool the potato salad to room temperature, cover it, and
refrigerate overnight.

Before serving this salad, toss it again, correct the seasoning, and
add more mayonnaise if it seems too dry.

soft tacos

BEEFY GUACAMOLE SOFT TACOS

Make the components earlier in the day; then at party time set the filling out in a colorful bowl, and let everyone fill their own tortilla. Messy but good!

1 tablespoon vegetable oil

1 small onion, chopped

1 pound ground beef

1 teaspoon salt

4 medium ripe avocados

1 cup sour cream

1/2 cup mayonnaise

1 (4-ounce) can diced green chiles

2 tablespoons fresh lime or lemon juice

1 teaspoon hot red pepper sauce, optional

3/4 teaspoon ground cumin

24 (6-inch) flour tortillas, heated in the oven

Fresh cilantro and chopped tomatoes for garnish

Heat the oil in a large skillet. Cook the onion over medium heat until softened. Add the ground beef, and season it with salt. Cook, stirring and breaking the meat into uniform crumbles, until the meat is lightly browned and just cooked through. Drain the cooked beef well, and let it cool. Refrigerate until ready to serve.

In a medium bowl, mash the avocados with a fork. Add the sour cream, mayonnaise, chiles, lime or lemon juice, hot sauce, if using, and cumin. Stir well. Cover and refrigerate up to 4 hours.

Just prior to serving, stir the beef-and-onion mixture into the guacamole. Serve with the tortillas, cilantro, and tomatoes.

LAYERED BEAN DIP

Does your crowd have a hearty appetite? Spread this Cal-Mex mixture in a great-looking platter, and surround it with tortilla chips.

1 (16-ounce) can Mexican-style refried beans
1 cup chunky prepared salsa, medium-hot or mild
1 small onion, grated
2 ripe Hass avocados
2 teaspoons fresh lemon juice
Pinch of salt and pepper
1 cup sour cream
1 cup grated Monterey Jack cheese
Taco chips or tortilla wedges, for scooping

Place the beans in a medium bowl, and mash them until they're softened. Add the salsa and grated onion, and mix well.

In a second bowl, mash the avocados with the lemon juice and salt and pepper. Blend until the mixture is smooth.

Spread the bean mixture in an 8-inch pan or serving dish. Spread the avocado mixture on top of the beans. Cover the avocado with a layer of sour cream. Sprinkle the cheese on top of the sour cream layer.

Serve immediately, or cover and chill for 2 hours. Serve the dip with crisp taco chips or wedges of flour tortillas.

block party activities

Even the most basic block party can benefit from some organized activities. Some of the wildest, best block parties I've learned about featured hilarious activities I would never have thought of: tractor races, street bowling, and water balloon tosses are just a few I've been introduced to. Other block parties have quiz sheets that are wonderful icebreakers. These communal activities can bring everyone together and provide some great entertainment and memories. Just make sure someone's got a camera.

If there are lots of kids, activities keep them busy and provide adults with some relief. In fact, if you have a lot of young ones, you may want to consider asking some teens to baby-sit, or run special games, a storytelling corner, or a puppet show. Make sure to enlist your volunteers well in advance.

Here are some activity suggestions:

◆ Water balloon toss

◆ Pig roast — it's a real focal point and a delicious change from burgers. There are companies who will bring the rotisserie and the beast. Be forewarned, though. A roasted pig looks a bit like a small dog and may upset some of the children — and some adults, too.

◆ Theme it — select a theme and let the food, the table decorations, and costumes reflect it. A popular movie might give you ideas, or go with a Hawaiian or musical theme. Vary the theme from year to year.

◆ Kids' talent show — let families know early on there will be a talent show. Each act should be no more than three minutes long. Encourage kids to hook up with one another and mix up the acts. Some might do a homegrown karaoke, or lip-sync performances, others might play an instrument or demonstrate pet tricks or magic tricks.

◆ A quiz sheet can be great entertainment. Ask neighbors to submit a surprising fact about themselves, something unusual that they have done in their lives. On the quiz sheet, list the accomplishment on the left side; on the right side list the mixed-up names. Everyone tries to match the name with the life event. Examples I've seen include: "I kissed a sea turtle." "I locked my dog in the car overnight." "I climbed Mount Everest."

◆ A pet show — let everyone know there will be a pet show contest, and see what shows up! One pet show had goofy prizes and ribbons for *any* pet that showed up — including the grandmother who brought her two grandchildren on a leash!

- Rent some fun. There are rental shops and party stores that will bring all kinds of entertainment, such as a miniature golf range, dunk tank, and a moon walk. They will set up and run this kids' entertainment for a few hundred bucks. If your block party is big enough and has a ton of kids, this may be just the hit-maker you need.

- Tractor race—in Guilford, Connecticut, one neighborhood races their fifteen sit-down tractors in three heats of five. Some even race with the snowplow attached; others pull a trailer!

- A new addition to one long-running block party is bowling. For the last six years, a Greenwood Avenue block party in Wilmette, Illinois, has concluded with street bowling, a game only adults get to play, but the kids love to watch. Someone on the block picked up a bowling ball and bag at a garage sale for three bucks, and a tradition was born. The ball is of medium weight, so everyone can handle it, and from years of street tossing it's chipped and scratched. But who cares? Everyone clears the block party chairs, and ten soda cans are arranged as pins. As the adults take their turns, some of the kids chase after the bowling ball while others reset the cans. The bowling bag is made of classic vinyl plaid, and each year the ball and bag go home with the winner for storage.

- Got a musical neighbor? Tap his or her talents. One block party I know of was not officially complete until one of the residents brought out his accordion and played. At another block party, in Brooklyn, one neighbor who plays in a jazz band invited some friends to come jam for the afternoon. Do you have a teenager who plays in a garage band? Bring on the band.

- In addition to these activities, ask someone to be the block party photographer. Digital cameras make it easy to take a load of pictures and to share them via e-mail, as well as to print them in different ways. Be sure to create an album that can chronicle your party over the years. Our block party has a book that chronicles thirty-five years of annual fun.

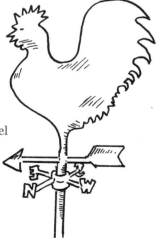

Keep in mind that a block party needs to make *everyone* feel included, and no one person should feel like he or she had to work during the entire event.

PEANUT BUTTER AND CHOCOLATE CRISPIE SQUARES

makes 36 pieces

No one can claim these will make you thin, but my husband, Todd, has perfected the recipe and I swear they are the very best Crispie squares ever. They freeze well, too.

$^1/_2$ cup (1 stick) butter

1 cup sugar

1 cup light corn syrup

1 cup creamy peanut butter

6 cups crisp rice cereal

topping

1 cup chocolate chips

$^1/_2$ cup butterscotch chips

3 tablespoons peanut butter

Melt the butter in a large saucepan. Add the sugar, corn syrup, and peanut butter and stir until smooth. Stir in all the rice cereal. Spread the mixture in an ungreased 9 × 12–inch pan.

In a double boiler, melt the chocolate chips. Add the butterscotch chips and peanut butter and blend well. Layer the melted chocolate mixture over the rice cereal mixture. Let cool. Cut into 1 × 2–inch pieces.

LIZA'S LEMON SQUARES

makes 16 squares

Pucker up! These tart treats disappear before any other dessert I make.

- 2 cups all-purpose flour
- $\frac{1}{2}$ cup confectioners' sugar, plus more for sprinkling
- $\frac{1}{2}$ pound (2 sticks) butter, melted
- 2 cups granulated sugar
- 1 teaspoon baking powder
- 4 large eggs, slightly beaten
- $\frac{1}{4}$ cup fresh lemon juice
- 1 tablespoon plus 1 teaspoon grated lemon zest

Preheat the oven to 350°F. Lightly grease a 9 x 12–inch baking pan.

Sift the flour and confectioners' sugar into a bowl. Add the melted butter, blend, and press the mixture into the pan. Bake the flour mixture for 20 minutes, or until it is just beginning to turn golden.

While the crust is baking, combine the sugar, baking powder, eggs, lemon juice, and lemon zest in a bowl. Pour the sugar mixture over the warm crust, and bake it for 25 more minutes. Cool the pastry on a rack. Cut it into squares, and chill. Before serving, sprinkle the lemon squares with confectioners' sugar. Store them in an airtight container.

MARBLE BLONDIES

marble blondies

makes 12 to 15 servings

Easy to make and easy to eat, these blond brownies are always a hit at the cookie exchange.

1	cup plus 2 tablespoons sifted flour
$1/2$	teaspoon baking soda
$1/2$	teaspoon salt
$1/2$	cup vegetable shortening
$1/4$	cup plus 2 tablespoons granulated sugar
$1/4$	cup plus 2 tablespoons brown sugar
$1/2$	teaspoon vanilla extract
$1/4$	teaspoon water
1	large egg
6	ounces chocolate chips

Preheat the oven to 375°F. Grease a 12 × 9 × 2–inch baking pan or glass dish.

Sift the flour, baking soda, and salt together.

In a mixer bowl, beat together the shortening, sugars, vanilla, and water. Beat in the egg. Add the flour mixture, and mix well.

Spread the batter in the pan, and sprinkle the chocolate chips over the top. Place the pan in the oven for 2 minutes to melt the chips; then drag a knife through the mixture to make a marbleized pattern.

Return the pan to the oven, and bake until browned: 10 to 12 minutes for an aluminum pan, or 12 to 14 minutes for a glass pan. Place the pan on a rack to cool, then cut the brownies into squares. Store the brownies in an airtight tin.

MOM'S BROWNIES

mom's brownies

makes 15 squares

I've made this one-pan brownie recipe for over twenty years. I have no idea why anyone would make brownies from a mix when it's this easy to make them from scratch.

4 squares unsweetened chocolate

1/2 pound (2 sticks) butter

4 eggs

2 cups sugar

1 1/2 cups flour

1 teaspoon baking soda

1/2 teaspoon salt

2 teaspoons vanilla extract

1 cup chopped walnuts, optional

Preheat the oven to 325°F. Grease a 9 × 12–inch baking pan.

Melt together the chocolate and butter in a medium saucepan. Remove the pan from the heat, and let the chocolate cool for 10 minutes. Beat in the eggs and sugar.

On a piece of waxed paper, mix the flour, baking soda, and salt. Add the flour mixture to the chocolate mixture, and mix. Add the vanilla and the walnuts, if using, and mix until the batter is blended.

Pour the batter into the prepared pan, and bake for 30 to 35 minutes, until a tester inserted in the center comes out almost clean. Cool the brownies on a rack. Cut them into squares. Store the brownies in an airtight tin.

Cut these up, layer them in waxed paper, and freeze for up to 3 months. They taste fresh-baked every time you thaw them.

ice cream cake

COFFEE ICE CREAM CAKE

makes 10 servings

Give yourself a day or two for this cake to freeze. You can use whichever ice cream flavors and mix-ins your crowd likes best.

6 ounces chocolate graham crackers (about 8)

3 tablespoons unsalted butter, melted

2 quarts coffee ice cream, slightly softened

2$^{1}/_{4}$ cups chilled heavy cream

$^{1}/_{2}$ teaspoon vanilla extract

1 cup plus 2 tablespoons confectioners' sugar

$^{1}/_{2}$ cup plus 1 tablespoon unsweetened cocoa powder

$^{1}/_{3}$ cup toffee pieces

Milk chocolate shavings, for serving

Chop the crackers in a food processor until they're finely ground. Add the melted butter, and process until the crumbs are moistened. Press the crumb mixture onto the bottom of a 9-inch springform pan. Freeze until the layer is firm, about 10 minutes.

Press the softened ice cream into the crust-lined pan, smooth the top, and cover the ice cream with plastic wrap. Freeze it overnight.

The next day, combine the heavy cream and vanilla in another large bowl. Sift the confectioners' sugar and cocoa over the cream. Using an electric mixer, beat until soft peaks form. Remove the plastic wrap from the frozen ice cream cake, and sprinkle the toffee bits on top. Cover with the whipped cream. Smooth and freeze until the whipped cream is set, at least 1 hour and up to 2 days.

To serve, sprinkle chocolate shavings over the cake. Run a knife between the pan sides and the cake to loosen it. Remove the pan sides. Using a small metal spatula or knife, smooth the cake sides. Let the cake stand at cool room temperature for 10 minutes before serving.

RANGER COOKIES

makes about 60 cookies

It wasn't a picnic around our house without a batch of these sturdy, crunchy cookies in the basket. Oatmeal, coconut, and flaked cereal give them their unique texture.

1 cup packed brown sugar

1 cup granulated sugar

1/2 pound (2 sticks) butter

2 large eggs

1 teaspoon vanilla extract

2 cups flour

2 teaspoons baking soda

1 1/2 teaspoons baking powder

1 teaspoon salt

1 cup oatmeal

1 cup sweetened, flaked coconut

1 cup bran or corn flakes

1 cup chocolate chips

Preheat the oven to 350°F. Lightly grease 1 or 2 cookie sheets.

In a large bowl, cream together the sugars and butter. Mix in the eggs and vanilla.

In another bowl, sift together the flour, baking soda, baking powder, and salt. Add to the sugar mixture, and blend thoroughly.

Stir in the oatmeal, coconut, cereal, and chocolate chips, and continue to mix until blended. The batter will be very stiff.

Drop the batter in tablespoon-size mounds onto the baking sheets. Bake until the cookies are lightly browned, about 10 to 12 minutes. Cool them on paper towels or a rack. Store the cookies in an airtight tin.

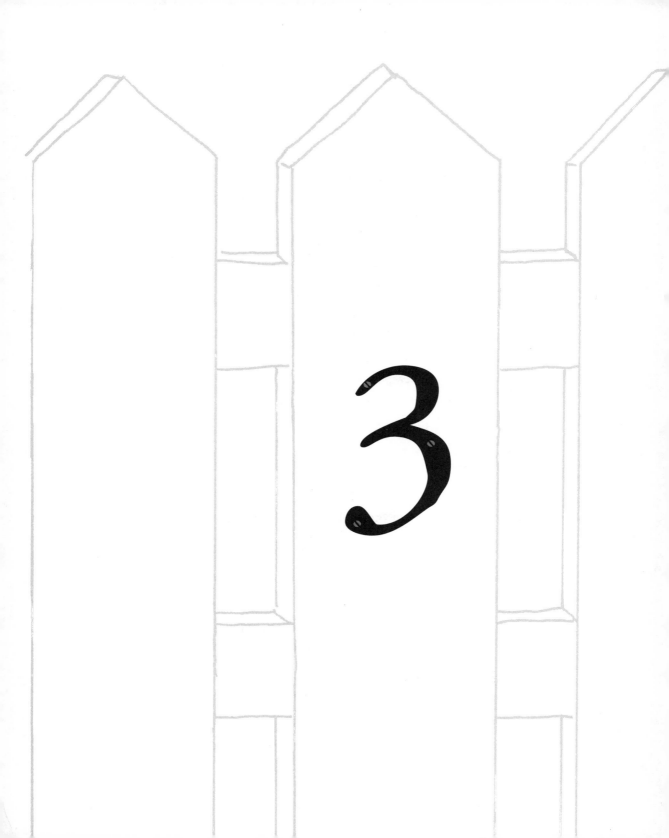

progressive dinners and other grown-ups-only events

As important as it is to come together as a neighborhood — moms, dads, kids, singles, grandparents, dogs, and all — once in a while it's nice to plan a gathering at which adult conversation can take center stage. With no need to supervise toddlers, amuse teens, or tailor activities to multigenerational interests, the adults in attendance can really relax, discuss topics of local concern, or just get silly without an audience.

1st Stop

Incredible Cheese Crisps 84

Buffalo Chicken Nuggets 85

Wild Rice Pancakes with Smoked Salmon 86

Broccoli Bites 88

Crab-and-Cheddar Crostini 89

Margaret's Cheese Board 90

Sun-Dried Tomato Tapenade 91

Golden Caviar Dip 92

Peel 'n' Eat Shrimp 93

Cold Cucumber-and-Potato Soup 94

Chilled Cantaloupe-Peach Soup 95

2nd Stop

Wisconsin Cassoulet 96

Chicken Thighs in Apple Cider 98

Indian Chicken with Tomatoes and Yogurt 100

Tuscan Chicken Rolls 102

Sautéed Chicken with Artichokes 104

Bridget Schroeder's Veal Stew 105

Savory Vegetable-and-Lamb Stew 106

Shrimp Creole 108

Roast Rosemary Potatoes with
Melted Cherry Tomatoes 110

Roasted Green Beans with Parmesan
and Pignolis 111

Pumpkin Risotto 112

Perfect Microwave Rice 113

3rd Stop

Blueberry Tart 114

"Cookie" Crust Tart 116

Better Than Pumpkin Pie 117

Chocolate Fondue with Fresh Fruit 118

Beyond Chip-and-Dip

Cheese Lace 119

Easy Chicken Empanadas 120

Pizza Bites 122

Potted Pecan Shrimp 123

Chicken Liver Mash 124

Warm Pizza Dip 125

Fried Potato Shells 130

Cheese Pillows 131

Smoked Oyster Dip 132

Crab-and-Jalapeño Dip 133

Cocomia Cookies 135

Grown-ups-only events tend to take place in the evenings when little ones are safely down for the night or at home with a sitter. (Some groups like to designate one home as the kids' depot, with an older child or two baby-sitting for the younger ones.) The gatherings themselves may revolve around food or have another focal point, such as a round of charades or a good old game of poker. Bunco parties have become popular across the country, and bridge has never gone out of style, but I've learned about many less-expected activities, from goofy costume parties to bowling competitions, that have become regular events in their areas. There are many excuses you can come up with to gather. Here are a few ideas.

◆ Death by Chocolate Night: This Valentine's Day party includes fine china, linen, and, of course, outrageous chocolate desserts.

◆ Wine Tasting: The host purchases three types of wine—cheap, modest, pricey. All three are set out in numbered tasting cups, and throughout the evening guests sample and vote on their favorite.

◆ Carp and Complain Night for Women: An impromptu excuse to unload, vent, and let off steam. This party usually takes place around the time that college applications are due, during long stretches of lousy weather, or after too many business trips have been taken. I'm told there's a rule: What gets said is forgotten by morning.

A comeback kid in the over-eighteen circuit is the progressive dinner, a movable feast potluck that takes place in three courses at three different homes over the course of a single night. Slightly more formal than your average covered-dish get-together, the progressive dinner allows a group of twenty or more to enjoy cocktails, a sit-down dinner, and a snazzy dessert buffet without leaving a host facing a mountain of dishes.

A side note here—there are people who love to set an elegant table and people whose "good" china hasn't been out of the closet since it was stowed there after the honeymoon. There is a place for both at neighborhood events. Be respectful of paper plates. They come in loads of colors and can look pretty dressed up on the right table. If a neighbor wants to use her china during a morning coffee, wonderful—though it doesn't commit you to do the same. To me a napkin is just something to wipe my fingers on, but I've been to some events where they were made from scratch for the party and tied up with clever napkin rings that were also made just for the occasion. Appreciate the effort, and skip any temptation to compare or judge.

But whether there's a three-course meal at the heart of your just-for-adults gathering or a bowl of chips and salsa, the right portable foods can make the event all the more enjoyable. The recipes in this chapter all travel well and have the sophisticated flavorings that please an adult palate. Try a few on the adults in your neck of the woods the next time you need a good excuse to get together for no good reason at all!

progressive dinners

Next to the block party, the progressive dinner is perhaps the most popular neighborhood event, and the trend is growing. I had never heard of progressive dinners until we moved to Rye, New York, where I read in our church bulletin that a progressive dinner was being organized. I was so naive I thought it was a political event and was surprised that the church was so much more liberal than I had imagined. Having now attended and hosted progressive dinners, I know they are evenings filled with good conversations, great food, and revolving settings.

If you're like most of us, the notion of preparing and serving a three-course meal to ten or more guests is a bit intimidating. The beauty of a progressive dinner is that using multiple venues spreads the workload, so that the hosting and cleanup duties are shared. The meal is divided into three courses: hors d'oeuvres, the main meal, and dessert, with each course served at a different home. From there, the variations begin. Some dinners have the host home do the cooking for that course, while other dinners treat all courses as a potluck and assign contributions. Because these are somewhat more formal events than those held outdoors, kids are not, as a rule, included. Progressive dinners often take place in the winter as a way to stay in touch despite busy schedules or cold weather. Once you've established the progressive dinner model in your community, you can use it for lots of different events throughout the year.

To get started, decide on the guest list. Unless you live in an area of particularly big homes, fifty to sixty people is about the limit. Like any neighborhood gathering, you must invite everyone in the immediate area, so no one feels they have been passed over. If your neighborhood is very extensive, consider holding two simultaneous events, again reducing the individual workload.

You will need to find three households to host a portion of the evening. If it's your idea, you better step up to the plate in the first year. At both the dessert house and the appetizer house you will only need room for people to mill around, but for the dinner course, ideally people should be able to sit while they eat.

Again, I found the two-invitation approach works well. Send out an anticipatory invitation explaining what a progressive dinner is and inviting folks to take part. Include a date and the time for each stage, for example: Appetizer Home, 6:30 P.M.; Dinner Home, 8:00 P.M.; Dessert Home, 9:30 P.M. If you have secured volunteers for host homes before the first invitation goes out, put their names and addresses on the invitation. Pick a Saturday or Sunday night that has the fewest number of conflicts. No date will be perfect, but steer clear of holidays, school vacations, and townwide events. Send this first invitation out well in advance, at least six weeks ahead. Follow up with the second one reminding everyone of the times and places.

Do not be discouraged if fewer people sign up than you thought. The first year is always the hardest, perhaps because some people think it sounds a little too different, and entering homes they aren't familiar with can put some people off. Go easy on the humor, and focus on how the party will work. Thanks to word of mouth, I promise you the second year's attendance will be terrific.

Remember, the name of the game is spreading the work, so be specific about what you need. Depending on the size of the group, you may want to break down the assignments so no one is cooking for the whole crowd. Here's a sample of what to request for a party of twenty couples:

- Appetizers: We need five volunteers to prepare one medium-size appetizer each.
- Main Course or Entrée: We need four volunteers to prepare an entrée for ten to twelve people.
- Extras: We need two volunteers to prepare a salad for thirty and to bring three loaves of bread each.
- Dessert: We need five volunteers to prepare a dessert that serves twelve.

Most people can swing an appetizer, and the local baker can bail you out of a dessert assignment, but many folks are intimidated by cooking a main dish. One way to take the pressure off is to provide the recipe for the main course and assign several people to make the same dish.

Some progressive-dinner organizers ask the host home to provide wine and beer. Alternatively, you could request donations to cover beverages, or assign them to noncooking guests. The key is to make everything easy and very clear.

the day of the party

Anyone preparing food should drop his or her dish off at the appropriate home before heading over to the appetizer house. Precooked entrées go to the entrée house with directions for reheating, if appropriate. Desserts go to the dessert house. Make sure your dish is labeled, and do the host a huge favor — make sure you come back the next day to retrieve your dish.

The evening starts at the appetizer house, and it is usually the appetizer host who reminds people when it's time to move to the next home, because that host will have scooted off a bit early to make sure all is ready.

Dinner is enjoyed at the second home, and dessert at the last home ends the evening. It's that simple, and it is the most fun you'll have with the least work!

INCREDIBLE CHEESE CRISPS

makes about 60 crisps

These make great nibbles. The mixture can be kept in the freezer and reheated in the microwave as needed. A batch in a freezer bag, complete with reheating instructions, makes a great hostess gift.

4 cups shredded sharp Cheddar cheese

2 cups all-purpose flour

2 cups very fresh crisp rice cereal

2 teaspoons sugar

$^1/_2$ teaspoon salt

$^1/_8$ teaspoon cayenne pepper

$^1/_8$ teaspoon dry mustard

$^1/_2$ pound (2 sticks) melted butter

Dash of Worcestershire sauce

Preheat the oven to 350°F.

In a large bowl, combine the cheese, flour, rice cereal, sugar, salt, cayenne, mustard, and melted butter, and add the Worcestershire. Toss until the ingredients are well blended, or blend with your hands.

Form the mixture into 1-inch balls, and arrange the balls an inch apart on an ungreased baking sheet. Flatten each ball with a fork, forming a crisscross pattern. The resulting disks should be about ¼ inch thick.

Bake until the edges are golden, about 10 to 12 minutes. Serve the cheese crisps warm or at room temperature. You can store them in sealable plastic bags in the freezer for up to 3 months.

BUFFALO CHICKEN NUGGETS

chicken nuggets

makes 32 servings

No neighborhood party is complete for my brother and sister-in-law without their Buffalo Chicken Nuggets. Connoisseurs of the standard buffalo wing, they came up with this boneless version years ago, and today it's the first thing to disappear at their neighborhood parties.

4 whole boneless, skinless chicken breasts (8 halves)

4 large eggs, beaten

$^{1}/_{2}$ cup flour

2 cups vegetable oil

1 12-ounce jar of Frank's Original Red Hot Cayenne Pepper Sauce, or other hot sauce

$^{1}/_{4}$ pound (1 stick) butter

$^{1}/_{2}$ cup packed brown sugar

Wash and cut off any excess fat from the chicken breasts. Cut the chicken into cubes. Dredge the cubes in the egg and then in the flour. Pour about ½ inch of oil into a deep frying pan. Heat the oil until it's very hot but not smoking. (If it's not hot enough, the flour won't stick to the chicken.)

Fry the chicken pieces until they're lightly brown and cooked through. Remove the nuggets with a slotted spoon, and drain them on paper towels.

In a deep saucepan, heat the hot sauce with the stick of butter until the butter melts. Add the brown sugar, 1 tablespoon at a time, to taste. If the sauce seems too spicy, add a little more brown sugar.

Place the chicken on a serving dish with a toothpick in each piece. Reheat the nuggets in the microwave for 2 minutes, or until hot. Serve the chicken with the dipping sauce.

WILD RICE PANCAKES WITH SMOKED SALMON

makes 24 servings as an appetizer

These elegant little appetizers are refined and rich. You can make the pancakes a day or two ahead and refrigerate them; bring to room temperature before serving.

1 tablespoon butter

1$\frac{1}{2}$ teaspoons salt

1 (6-ounce) package long-grain and wild rice

2 large eggs

1 tablespoon olive oil

2 tablespoons all-purpose flour

4 scallions, finely chopped

1$\frac{1}{2}$ teaspoons fresh thyme (or $\frac{1}{2}$ teaspoon dried)

$\frac{1}{8}$ teaspoon fresh ground pepper

$\frac{1}{4}$ to $\frac{1}{3}$ cup peanut or corn oil

1 cup sour cream

3 ounces thinly sliced smoked salmon, cut into strips

Chives, dill, cilantro, or capers for garnish

In a medium saucepan, combine the butter, salt, and 2$\frac{1}{3}$ cups of water over medium heat. Stir in the rice, discarding the seasoning packet. Bring the mixture to a boil, cover it, and simmer over low heat until the rice is tender, about 25 minutes. Drain the rice and let it cool for 5 minutes.

In a medium bowl, beat the eggs with the olive oil until blended. Mix in the flour. Stir in the scallions, thyme, and pepper until well mixed. Stir in the cooked rice and combine thoroughly.

In a large frying pan, warm 2 tablespoons of the peanut oil over medium heat. Drop tablespoons of the rice mixture into the hot pan, and flatten the pancakes with the back of a spoon.

Cook, turning once, until the pancakes are browned on both sides, about 4 minutes total. Drain them on paper towels. Repeat with the rest of the "batter," adding more oil to the pan as necessary. Cool to room temperature, or wrap well and refrigerate for up to 2 days.

Serve 2 pancakes on a small plate at room temperature topped with 1 tablespoon of sour cream, a sliver of salmon, and any of the garnishes of your choice.

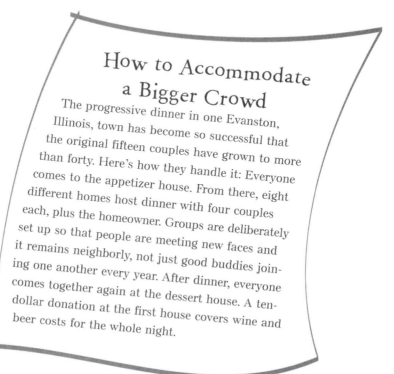

How to Accommodate a Bigger Crowd

The progressive dinner in one Evanston, Illinois, town has become so successful that the original fifteen couples have grown to more than forty. Here's how they handle it: Everyone comes to the appetizer house. From there, eight different homes host dinner with four couples each, plus the homeowner. Groups are deliberately set up so that people are meeting new faces and it remains neighborly, not just good buddies joining one another every year. After dinner, everyone comes together again at the dessert house. A ten-dollar donation at the first house covers wine and beer costs for the whole night.

BROCCOLI BITES

makes 24 servings as an hors d'oeuvre

This is a good "freeze 'em till you need 'em" appetizer. Use a small ice cream scoop or two spoons to quickly form these zesty balls onto parchment paper. Stack the sheets in your freezer; then slide each sheet onto a baking sheet.

2 (10-ounce) packages frozen chopped broccoli

2 cups herb stuffing mix

1 cup grated Parmesan cheese

6 large eggs, beaten

1 1/2 teaspoons cayenne pepper

1/4 pound plus 4 tablespoons (1 1/2 sticks) butter, softened

1/2 teaspoon salt

1/4 teaspoon pepper

Cook the broccoli according to the package directions, and drain well. Combine the broccoli in a medium bowl with the stuffing mix, cheese, eggs, cayenne pepper, butter, salt, and black pepper. Mix the ingredients well. Roll the mixture into 1-inch balls.

Place the balls in a single layer on parchment paper sheets that fit stacked in your freezer. Freeze them for at least 3 hours. The balls are now ready to be stored in heavy plastic bags in the freezer for up to 2 months.

To serve, preheat the oven to 350°F. Transfer the broccoli bites with the parchment paper to a cookie sheet, and bake until they're browned, about 15 minutes.

crostini

CRAB-AND-CHEDDAR CROSTINI

makes 36 servings as an hors d'oeuvre

Your guests will be rolling on the floor in ecstasy when they taste these decadent treats.

1 pint fresh crabmeat

1 cup mayonnaise

1 cup grated Cheddar cheese

2 tablespoons chopped fresh chives or scallions

1 teaspoon fresh lemon juice

$^1/_8$ teaspoon freshly ground cayenne pepper

36 thin baguette slices

Preheat the oven to 400°F. Pick through the crabmeat, and discard any bits of shell or cartilage.

In a medium bowl, combine the mayonnaise, Cheddar, chives, lemon juice, and cayenne. Mix until well blended. Gently fold in the crab. Lay the baguette slices in a single layer on a baking sheet, and spread each slice evenly with about 1 tablespoon of the crab mixture.

Bake until the crostini are golden brown and bubbly, 5 to 7 minutes. Serve warm.

MARGARET'S CHEESE BOARD

makes 12 to 16 squares

Buy the best Cheddar you can find. Your house will smell great when the first neighbors hit the door!

$^1/_4$ pound (1 stick) butter

1 cup chopped onions

$1^1/_2$ cups biscuit baking mix (such as Bisquick)

1 cup milk

1 large egg

3 ounces sharp Cheddar cheese, grated

Poppy seeds, for sprinkling

Preheat the oven to 400°F.

Melt 4 tablespoons of the butter in a skillet. Add the onions, and sauté them until they're softened and beginning to color, 6 to 8 minutes.

In a mixing bowl, combine the biscuit mix, milk, egg, half the grated cheese, and the sautéed onions. Mix until the batter is lumpy.

Grease a 9 × 13–inch pan, pour the batter into it, and scatter the rest of the cheese on top. Melt the remaining butter, and drizzle it over the cheese; then sprinkle with poppy seeds. Bake for 20 to 25 minutes. Cut the cheese board into squares, and serve it warm.

SUN-DRIED TOMATO TAPENADE

makes ¹/₂ cup

Serve this concoction in a crock, alongside crostini or a thin-sliced baguette.
The potent Mediterranean flavors are also yummy on slices of boiled potato.
Make it a day ahead to let the flavors blend.

12 black brine-cured olives (such as Kalamata),
   pitted

9 sun-dried tomatoes in oil, well drained and
   coarsely chopped

¹/₄ cup minced fresh Italian parsley

2 tablespoons tomato paste

1 teaspoon balsamic vinegar

1 teaspoon chopped fresh thyme

1 small garlic clove, minced

Salt to taste

Mix all the ingredients in a food processor until finely chopped and
well blended. Season to taste with salt. Cover it well, and refrigerate for at least 24 hours.

The tapenade keeps for a week in the refrigerator.

GOLDEN CAVIAR DIP

makes about 2 cups

Who says caviar is beyond your budget? Our version is elegant *and* inexpensive! Serve this in a bowl with crudités, or put a dab of dip on cucumber rounds or endive spears and pass them around on a tray.

- 1 (4-ounce) jar golden caviar
- ½ cup extra virgin olive oil
- ½ cup sour cream
- 3 finely chopped green onions
- 2 tablespoons vodka
- 2 teaspoons ketchup
- 2 teaspoons fresh lime juice

Gently whisk the caviar in a medium bowl until the eggs begin to separate. Add the oil slowly, in a steady stream, whisking until the oil is fully incorporated.

Fold in the sour cream. Stir in the remaining ingredients until the mixture is well blended. Serve this dip slightly chilled. It can be refrigerated, covered, for up to 2 days.

PEEL 'N' EAT SHRIMP

makes 8 to 12 servings

This crowd-pleaser also gives folks a little fun work to do!

10 whole peppercorns

2 pounds small or medium raw shrimp, unpeeled

2 bay leaves

cocktail sauce

1 cup ketchup

2 tablespoons prepared horseradish

Dash of Tabasco or other hot sauce

1 tablespoon fresh lemon juice, or to taste

Bring 2 quarts of water to a rolling boil. Add the peppercorns. Add the shrimp and bay leaves all at once, and set the timer for 1 minute; boil the shrimp until the timer rings or just until they turn pink all over. Drain the shrimp immediately, and run cold water over them so they won't continue to cook. Refrigerate the cooked shrimp in a bowl with ice cubes.

Combine the cocktail sauce ingredients in a small bowl, and blend them well. Refrigerate the sauce for at least an hour (and up to 3 days) to allow the flavors to develop.

Serve the chilled shrimp with the cocktail sauce and a bowl to catch the peelings.

COLD CUCUMBER-AND-POTATO SOUP

makes 6 to 8 servings

A little lighter than vichyssoise, this soup has much less fat. This recipe can be doubled or tripled.

2 teaspoons vegetable oil

1 medium onion, coarsely chopped (about ¾ cup)

2 cups diced, peeled cucumbers

1⅓ cups diced, peeled potatoes

2 cups chicken broth

1 cup water

Salt to taste

Pepper to taste

1 tablespoon chopped fresh dill

Fresh dill sprigs for garnish

Heat the oil in a large saucepan. Add the onion and cucumbers, and stir them with a large spoon. Cover and cook the vegetables over low heat until the cucumbers lose their crispness, about 10 minutes. Add the potatoes, broth, water, salt, and pepper, cover the saucepan, and bring the soup to a boil. Reduce the heat and simmer, covered, until the vegetables are tender, about 10 minutes. Remove the soup from the heat and let it stand uncovered to cool somewhat.

In batches, transfer the soup to a food processor. Add the dill, and process until the mixture is almost smooth. Pour the soup into a container, and cover and chill it. Serve this soup cold, garnished with fresh dill sprigs.

CHILLED CANTALOUPE-PEACH SOUP

makes 6 servings

A cold, sweet soup is a delightful way to begin a hot summer night's meal. Make this when the peaches are at their delectable best, and make sure the melon is very ripe. It looks great served in a balloon wine goblet.

6 ripe peaches

$\frac{1}{2}$ cup dry white wine

$\frac{1}{4}$ cup plus 2 tablespoons fresh lemon juice

1 tablespoon honey

$\frac{1}{4}$ teaspoon cinnamon

Dash of nutmeg

1 medium cantaloupe, peeled

1 cup fresh orange juice

Blueberries, for garnish

Bring a saucepan of water to a boil. Dip the peaches in the boiling water for 5 to 10 seconds to loosen the skins; then pit and slice them. Discard the water, and return the peaches to the saucepan with the wine, lemon juice, honey, cinnamon, and nutmeg. Heat to a boil, lower the heat, cover, and simmer for 10 minutes. Cool the peach mixture to room temperature. Transfer the cooked peach mixture to a food processor, and puree until it is smooth. Transfer it to a mixing bowl.

Cut approximately ¾ of the cantaloupe into chunks, and place the chunks in the food processor. Puree the cantaloupe with the orange juice until smooth; then stir it into the peach puree. Cut what remains of the melon into ¼-inch cubes, and add it to the soup. Cover and chill the soup for at least 3 hours.

Serve this soup very cool, garnished with blueberries.

WISCONSIN CASSOULET

wisconsin cassoulet

makes 8 to 10 servings

Linda Gartz welcomed us to town with this terrific dish. Created by Sandi Hillmer of Muskego, Wisconsin, this hearty potful serves a crowd and is loaded with flavor. It's perfect for blustery winter nights, to warm your guests as they come in from the cold.

1   pound dried navy beans

4   celery hearts (about top 3 inches) with leaves

2   bay leaves

2   sprigs fresh Italian parsley

1/4   pound slab bacon, rind removed, cut into 1/4-inch dice

1/4   cup extra virgin olive oil, or more if necessary

3   skinless, boneless chicken breast halves (about 5 ounces each), cut into 1 1/2-inch pieces

1   boneless pork loin (about 3 pounds), cut into 1 1/2-inch pieces

1   cup chopped onions

1/4   cup chopped celery

1/4   cup chopped carrots

3   garlic cloves, minced (1 1/2 teaspoons)

3   cups chicken broth

1   (28-ounce) can Italian plum tomatoes, undrained, coarsely chopped

1/3   cup pure maple syrup

1/4   cup packed light brown sugar

1   teaspoon dried thyme

1/4   teaspoon dried savory

1/4   teaspoon dry mustard

1/4   teaspoon cracked black pepper

1/2   pound kielbasa sausage, cut into 1 1/2-inch pieces

1/4   cup chopped fresh flat-leaf parsley, plus 3 tablespoons for garnish

2   teaspoons salt, or to taste

Pick over the beans, discarding any stones. Soak the beans overnight in enough cold water to cover them by 2 inches. Rinse the beans in several changes of cold water, and drain them well.

Place the soaked beans in a large heavy pot, and add enough water to cover them. Add the celery tops, bay leaves, and parsley sprigs. Simmer for 30 minutes over medium heat.

While the beans cook, place the bacon in a very large stew pot over medium-low heat, and cook until it is golden brown and fat is rendered, about 6 to 8 minutes. Remove the bacon with a slotted spoon, and set it aside.

Add 2 tablespoons of the olive oil to the pot, and brown the chicken and the pork in batches until the meat is golden on all sides, about 5 to 6 minutes per batch. Using a slotted spoon, transfer the meat to a bowl, and set it aside.

Add the rest of the oil to the pot, and cook the onions, chopped celery, and carrots over medium-low heat until the celery is wilted, 8 to 10 minutes. Return the browned meat and bacon to the pot, along with the beans (but discard celery tops). Add the garlic, broth, tomatoes, syrup, brown sugar, and all the dried herbs and spices.

Simmer, stirring occasionally, for 1 hour. Add the kielbasa, and continue to simmer, stirring once or twice, until all is cooked through, about 30 minutes.

Remove and discard the parsley sprigs and bay leaves from the cassoulet. Stir in the chopped parsley, and season with the salt. Serve this dish immediately, garnished with the remaining chopped parsley.

CHICKEN THIGHS
IN APPLE CIDER

Here's another great harvest dish you can make at your leisure and then heat up just before serving. Chicken thighs are the forgotten chicken meat, which is a shame, as they are far more tender and flavorful than any other part. Occasionally you will find boneless, skinless thighs at the market. Buy them all and freeze them. They are so good, and someone else has done all the deboning work!

Olive oil, to coat skillet

24 chicken thighs, with skin

Flour for dredging

9 tablespoons (approximately) extra virgin olive oil

3 large onions, diced (about 1 1/2 cups)

9 carrots, diced

6 tablespoons butter

6 Granny Smith apples, peeled, cored, and cut into eighths

3 tablespoons curry powder

3 tablespoons flour

3/4 cup applejack (hard cider brandy)

1 1/2 cups apple cider

1 1/2 cups hot chicken stock

Preheat the oven to 350°F.

Heat an ovenproof skillet or casserole (make sure it has a tight-fitting lid) over medium heat with 3 tablespoons of olive oil. Dredge the chicken pieces in flour, shaking off the excess. Add 6 to 8 thighs to the skillet, skin side down, and brown them well before turning to brown the other side. When the chicken is well browned, remove it and set it aside. Coat the skillet with more olive oil, and continue to brown the thighs in batches.

Add the onions to the casserole, and cook them over medium heat to a golden brown, about 5 minutes, before adding the carrots. Cook the carrots for 2 to 3 minutes.

In a separate skillet, melt 2 tablespoons of the butter and add ⅓ of the sliced apples. Brown both sides of the slices over medium heat. When done, add to the carrots and onions. Repeat 2 more times.

Sprinkle the curry powder and flour over the vegetables and apples. Stir to combine well, and toast the vegetable combination for 1 minute.

Add the chicken to the pan and, removing the pan from the heat for a moment, carefully pour in the applejack. Let the brandy bubble and begin to evaporate in the hot casserole before returning it to the heat.

Preheat the oven to 350°F. Add the apple cider and chicken stock, bring the mixture quickly to a boil, reduce the heat to a slow simmer, cover the pan with a tight-fitting lid, and place the pan in the oven for 35 minutes. When the chicken is fully cooked, remove it from the oven, carefully ladle off any grease, and serve it with the apple slices.

VARIATION

Substitute 2 pears for the apples. Use Poir William (pear brandy) and pear nectar instead of the applejack and cider.

INDIAN CHICKEN WITH TOMATOES AND YOGURT

indian chicken

makes 6 servings

This dish has won raves at a progressive dinner where cultural diversity is celebrated. It is much easier to make than the long list of ingredients would suggest—it's quite economical, too, and easily doubled. This dish can be made a day in advance. Cool, cover, and refrigerate it. To serve, heat the chicken gently and stir. Serve this meal with steamed white rice, preferably basmati.

1/4 cup vegetable oil

3/4 teaspoon whole cumin seeds

1 cinnamon stick

6 whole cardamom pods

2 bay leaves

2 yellow onions, finely chopped

6 garlic cloves, chopped

1 -inch piece fresh ginger, finely chopped

6 cloves

1 teaspoon ground coriander

1/4 teaspoon ground turmeric

1/4 teaspoon cayenne pepper

1 1/2 teaspoons salt

2 to 3 medium tomatoes, chopped (or one 14 1/2-ounce can diced tomatoes)

1 (6- to 8-ounce) can tomato sauce

3 pounds boneless, skinless chicken breasts cut into 2-inch cubes

1/4 cup plain yogurt, fork-whipped

Juice of 1 lemon

1/2 cup fresh cilantro leaves, chopped

Heat the oil in a large nonstick pot over medium-high heat. When the pan is hot, add the cumin seeds, cinnamon, cardamom, and bay leaves. As soon as they begin to sizzle and become fragrant (just a few seconds) add the onions, garlic, and ginger. Stir until the onions turn golden and soft, 5 minutes.

Add the cloves, coriander, turmeric, cayenne, and salt, and stir for a few more minutes. Add the tomatoes and tomato sauce. Stir, reduce the heat to low, cover the pan, and simmer for 4 minutes.

Raise the heat to medium, add the chicken pieces, and sauté them for a few minutes. Stir in the yogurt, reduce the heat to low, cover the pan, and simmer for 30 minutes, until the chicken is tender, stirring occasionally. Remove the cover, turn the heat up to medium, and let some of the liquid evaporate. Stir in the lemon juice and cilantro just before serving.

Valentine Dinner

One progressive dinner I learned of was in celebration of Valentine's Day. Prior to coming to the appetizer house, guests were asked to drop off a baby picture of themselves at the dessert house. The evening ended with people trying to guess which guest belonged to which picture.

TUSCAN CHICKEN ROLLS

tuscan
chicken rolls

makes 8 to 10 servings

Food Network's Susan Stockton contributed this fantastic stuffed chicken dish, which makes for a beautiful presentation. Accompany it with roasted potatoes and a big salad.

8 boneless, skinless chicken breasts

8 slices prosciutto

1 pound Fontina cheese, cut into sticks of about $1/2 \times 3$ inches

1 red bell pepper (or 1 large jar of roasted peppers), cored, seeded, and sliced into thin strips

1 pound thin asparagus, trimmed to 3-inch lengths and blanched in boiling salted water for 2 minutes and then dropped into ice water

$1/2$ cup chopped Italian parsley

$1/4$ cup chopped fresh tarragon

1 pint sour cream

3 cups coarse, dry corn-bread crumbs or regular bread crumbs (or both)

3 tablespoons dry mustard

$3/4$ cup grated Parmesan cheese

Salt and pepper

3 cups inexpensive balsamic vinegar

1 tablespoon brown sugar

Preheat the oven to 400°F. Use a pounder or a heavy skillet to flatten each chicken breast to about ½ inch thick. Try to make each piece as wide as you can.

Gather all the other ingredients for assembly: prosciutto, Fontina sticks, red pepper strips, blanched asparagus, and chopped herbs. Place the sour cream in a shallow bowl; in another shallow bowl combine the corn-bread crumbs, dry mustard, Parmesan, and salt and pepper.

Lay the chicken breasts on the work surface and then top each one with a piece of prosciutto. Center the strips of cheese and peppers and the asparagus across each breast. Sprinkle the breasts with the herbs. Pull on the sides of each breast to encase the cheese mixture; then roll each breast up over the filling and secure the roll with a toothpick.

Dip each roll into sour cream, covering it liberally. (This is messy; try to use one hand only.) Drop the roll into the second bowl, and use your clean hand to dredge the rolls in seasoned crumbs. Place the breaded rolls seam side down on a baking sheet.

Bake the rolls for 45 minutes, or until golden and cooked through. Meanwhile, in a small saucepan over medium-high heat, reduce the balsamic vinegar and brown sugar until ¾ cup remains.

After baking, allow the chicken rolls to stand for 10 minutes. Slice the rolls into 1-inch pieces, arrange them on dinner plates, and drizzle with the balsamic glaze.

SAUTÉED CHICKEN WITH ARTICHOKES

This elegant meal is really a one-pot dish (not counting the rice) that takes only a half hour from stove to table.

3 pounds boneless chicken breasts or thighs

4 tablespoons ($^1/_2$ stick) butter

$^1/_4$ cup extra virgin olive oil

6 garlic cloves, minced (about 1 tablespoon)

Freshly ground black pepper

4 large coarsely chopped tomatoes or 1 (28-ounce) can

3 cans halved artichoke hearts

2 cups ripe olive halves

$^1/_2$ cup plus 2 tablespoons chopped Italian parsley

$^1/_2$ cup dry white wine

4 cups cooked rice

Pound the chicken between two sheets of waxed paper or plastic wrap to a ¼-inch thickness. Cut the pounded chicken into 2- to 3-inch squares. In a large sauté pan, heat the butter and oil over low heat. When the butter has melted, add the garlic, and stir it for about 1 minute; then turn the heat to medium-high. Sauté the chicken in small batches in a single layer until just cooked, about 6 to 8 minutes per side. Transfer the cooked pieces to a plate.

Return all the cooked chicken to the pan, plus any juices remaining on the plate, and sprinkle with pepper. Add the tomatoes and artichokes. Cook for 3 minutes; then add the olives and parsley, and mix thoroughly. Continue to cook, stirring once in a while, for 12 to 15 minutes more, adding the wine in the last 2 minutes. Serve the chicken over rice.

BRIDGET SCHROEDER'S VEAL STEW

makes 6 to 8 servings

This has been a hit at an Evanston, Illinois, progressive dinner for more than five years. The recipe doubles very well. This stew can be partially baked and finished in the oven of the dinner host or fully baked and kept warm in a 200°F oven. Make sure it is tightly covered so it does not dry out if the cocktail hour goes longer than expected. Bridget likes to serve it over a mixture of wild and long-grain rice, but polenta would be nice, too.

- 1/2 cup extra virgin olive oil
- 3 onions, halved and sliced
- 3 garlic cloves, minced (1 1/2 teaspoons)
- 2 pounds veal stew meat, cubed
- 4 strips orange zest, white pith removed
- 3 carrots, julienned
- 1 (28-ounce) can whole plum tomatoes with juice
- 1 cup dry white wine
- 3/4 teaspoon dried thyme
- 3/4 teaspoon rosemary
- 1/4 cup quartered black olives, for garnish

Preheat the oven to 325°F.

Heat the olive oil in a deep casserole or lidded, ovenproof pot. Add the onions and garlic, and sauté until they're softened, 6 to 8 minutes. Add the veal, orange zest, carrots, tomatoes and their juices, wine, thyme, and rosemary, and mix well. Cover and bake for 1½ to 2 hours, until the meat is very tender.

Garnish the stew with the olives, and serve it over rice or polenta.

SAVORY VEGETABLE -AND- LAMB STEW

makes 8 to 10 servings

The beauty of this dish is how well it travels. Make it early in the day, and reheat it just before serving, and the flavor will be even better.

1 tablespoon plus 1 teaspoon extra virgin olive oil

2 pounds lean boneless lamb stew meat, from the shoulder or leg, cut into 2-inch chunks

Salt and freshly ground pepper

1 large onion, cut lengthwise into 8 wedges

1 cinnamon stick

$^1/_2$ teaspoon ground turmeric

Pinch of crumbled saffron threads (optional)

1 quart chicken stock or canned low-sodium chicken broth

6 medium carrots, quartered lengthwise and halved crosswise

3 large celery ribs, halved lengthwise and quartered crosswise

5 small zucchini, halved lengthwise and crosswise

10 small pattypan squash, trimmed

2 (15-ounce) cans chickpeas, drained and rinsed

Minced parsley, for garnish

Heat 1 tablespoon of the olive oil in a large heavy saucepan. Generously season the lamb with the salt and pepper. Working in 3 batches, sauté the meat over moderately high heat until browned all over, about 5 minutes per batch. Transfer the meat to a platter.

Add the remaining 1 teaspoon of the oil to the saucepan, and cook the onion wedges over moderate heat, turning once, until they are browned on both sides, about 4 minutes. Transfer the onion wedges to the platter.

Return the meat to the saucepan. Add the cinnamon stick, turmeric, saffron, chicken stock, and 1 quart of water, and bring the mixture to a simmer over high heat. Reduce the heat to moderately low, and simmer until the meat is tender, about 1 hour. Add the carrots, celery, and onion wedges to the saucepan, and return it to a simmer. Cook until the carrots are almost tender, about 15 minutes. Add the zucchini, pattypan squash, and chickpeas, and cook until the zucchini and squash are just tender, about 10 minutes longer.

Discard the cinnamon stick, and season the stew with salt and pepper. Serve garnished with minced parsley.

SHRIMP CREOLE

shrimp creole

This progressive-dinner dish is now a standard in one neighborhood. It's based on a classic Paul Prudhomme recipe, simplified for ease of preparation. It's still delicious.

1/4 cup vegetable oil (can use frozen fish stock and dilute per package instructions)

2 1/2 cups finely chopped onions

1 3/4 cups finely chopped celery

1 1/2 cups finely chopped green peppers

4 tablespoons unsalted butter

2 teaspoons minced garlic (4 medium cloves)

1 bay leaf

2 teaspoons salt

1 1/2 teaspoons white pepper

1 teaspoon cayenne pepper

3/4 teaspoon black pepper

1 1/2 teaspoons Tabasco sauce

1 tablespoon dried thyme leaves

1 1/2 teaspoons dried basil leaves

2 1/2 cups fish stock

1 (14 1/2-ounce) can diced tomatoes

1 (14-ounce) can toamto sauce (1 1/2 cups)

2 teaspoons sugar

3 1/2 pounds medium or large shrimp, peeled and deveined

5 cups hot cooked rice

Heat the oil or fat at high heat in a 4-quart saucepan. Add 1 cup of the onions, and cook over high heat for 3 minutes, stirring frequently, until the onions are a rich brown color but not burned, about 3 to 5 minutes. Add the remaining 1½ cups of onions, the celery, green peppers, and butter. Cook over high heat until the peppers and celery start to get tender, about 5 minutes, stirring occasionally. Add the garlic, bay leaf, salt, and all the peppers, and stir well. Then add the Tabasco, thyme, basil, and ½ cup of the stock. Cook over medium heat for about 5 minutes to allow the seasonings to marry and the vegetables to brown further, stirring occasionally and scraping the bottom of the pan. Stir in the tomato sauce, and simmer 5 minutes, stirring occasionally. Add the remaining 2 cups of stock and the sugar. Continue simmering for 15 minutes, stirring the sauce occasionally. (The creole sauce can be cooled for up to 24 hours. Bring it back to a boil before continuing with the recipe.)

Remove the sauce from the heat, and add the shrimp. Cover the pot, and let it sit just until the shrimp are plump and pink, about 5 to 10 minutes. Serve immediately. Put ½ cup of rice in the center of the plate, spoon 1 cup Shrimp Creole sauce around the rice, and arrange 8 to 9 shrimp on the sauce.

Take a Seat

Try to set up the dinner house so that people can sit at tables instead of eating from their laps if you can possibly swing it. It may require borrowing lawn furniture, piano benches, and stools from here and there, but it really makes conversations flow better if no one has to juggle plate, cutlery, and wineglass while eating. And use every square inch of floor space. When I hosted dinner, I had borrowed folding tables everywhere, including the hallways, and I borrowed chairs from three different houses on the block.

ROAST ROSEMARY POTATOES WITH MELTED CHERRY TOMATOES

makes 8 to 10 servings

2 pounds new potatoes

1 small bunch fresh rosemary

1/4 cup olive oil

Coarse salt

1 tablespoon olive oil

2 garlic cloves

2 pints cherry tomatoes

1/4 cup fresh thyme leaves

Preheat the oven to 400°F.

Quarter the potatoes; then place them in a roasting pan large enough to hold them in one layer. Strip the leaves from the rosemary branches, and toss the leaves into the roasting pan. Drizzle the potatoes and rosemary with ¼ cup olive oil. Toss the potatoes well and sprinkle them liberally with coarse salt. Roast for 40 minutes, or until the potatoes are tender inside and browned outside.

Warm a medium skillet over high heat. Add the oil, and cook the garlic cloves until golden. Remove and discard the garlic; then add the cherry tomatoes to the pan. Cook, shaking the pan, until the tomato skins split and the juices flow. Sprinkle with the thyme, and serve.

ROASTED GREEN BEANS WITH PARMESAN AND PIGNOLIS

makes 8 to 10 servings

You can refrigerate the parboiled beans for a day or two; a quick trip to the oven is all you'll need to do on party night. And you can cook a lot at once.

2 pounds green beans, ends trimmed

¼ cup pignolis (pine nuts)

Salt

Black pepper to taste

2 tablespoons olive oil

½ cup coarsely grated Parmesan cheese

Preheat the oven to 350°F.

Bring a large pot of water to a boil. Add the beans and cook about 5 minutes, or until just barely tender. Drain well.

Spread the pignolis on a baking sheet with sides and toast in the oven until just browned, about 7 minutes. Set aside to cool.

Toss the beans with the oil on the baking sheet. Season with salt and pepper and roast in the oven for 10–12 minutes, or until slightly wilted. Transfer to a serving bowl and toss with the Parmesan and the pignolis. Serve warm.

PUMPKIN RISOTTO

My sister serves this pretty fall dish in mini pumpkins that she hollows out and bakes in a 450°F oven until they are tender. Either this way or in bowls, it's a showstopper.

5¼ cups chicken broth

1½ cups water

1 medium onion, chopped (about 1½ cups)

3 large garlic cloves, thinly sliced

1 tablespoon minced

4 tablespoons unsalted butter

1½ cups Arborio or other short-grain rice

¾ cup dry white wine

1 (15-ounce) can pumpkin puree

¼ cup plus 2 tablespoons chopped fresh chives

salt and pepper

Chopped fresh chives

Parmesan cheese curls shaved with a vegetable peeler from a ¼-pound piece of Parmesan

Preheat the oven to 450°F.

In a saucepan, combine the broth and water, and bring to a simmer. Keep at a bare simmer.

In another saucepan, cook the onion, garlic, and ginger in butter over moderately low heat, stirring, until the vegetables are softened. Stir in the rice and cook over moderate heat, stirring constantly, about 1 minute. Add the wine, and cook, stirring, until it is absorbed. Stir in ¼ cup of the hot diluted broth, and cook, stirring constantly and keeping the mixture at a simmer throughout, until the broth is absorbed.

Continue simmering and adding broth, about ¼ cup at a time, stirring constantly and letting each addition be absorbed before adding the next, until about half the broth has been added. Stir in the pumpkin, and continue simmering and adding broth in same manner until the rice is tender and creamy-looking but still al dente, about 18 minutes total. Stir in the chopped chives and salt and pepper to taste.

Garnish the risotto with chives and Parmesan curls.

PERFECT MICROWAVE RICE

rice

makes 4 cups

This is not a faster way to prepare this flavorful rice, just a foolproof one.

2 cups basmati rice

3 cups water

Stir the rice together with the water in a deep microwave-safe serving dish. Cover the rice and microwave it on HIGH for 15 minutes. Uncover the rice and microwave it on HIGH for 5 additional minutes. Let it stand for another 5 minutes.

Fluff the rice with a fork, and serve it immediately.

Why Three When You Could Do Four?

On Johnnycake Lane in Averill Park, New York, progressive dinners include a fourth stop—a soup course. And at another dinner, I learned that their fourth stop is at a home with a large foyer where everyone gathers for a little post-prandial dancing.

BLUEBERRY TART

makes 12 servings

Combining cooked and raw berries complicates the flavor and improves the texture of this North Woods summer favorite.

crust

1¼ cups all-purpose flour

¼ cup sugar

¼ teaspoon salt

¼ pound (1 stick) cold unsalted butter, cut into bits

1 large egg yolk

filling

3 tablespoons water

1 envelope unflavored gelatin

1 tablespoon fresh lemon juice

½ cup sugar

¼ teaspoon ground cinnamon

Pinch of salt

8 cups fresh blueberries

1 tablespoon vanilla extract

Whipped cream, for serving

In a food processor, blend together the flour, sugar, salt, and butter until the mixture resembles coarse meal. Add the egg yolk and pulse until the dough begins to come together but is still crumbly.

Press the dough evenly onto the bottom and up the sides of an 11-inch tart pan with a removable fluted rim. Chill the crust for 30 minutes.

Preheat the oven to 400°F. Prick the bottom of the crust all over with a fork. Bake the crust in the middle of the oven for 20 to 25 minutes, or until golden. Cool it in the pan on a rack.

Pour the water into a small bowl, and sprinkle the gelatin over the water to soften. Combine the lemon juice, sugar, cinnamon, salt, and 3 cups of the berries in a saucepan, and simmer, stirring occasionally, for 10 minutes. Remove the pan from the heat, and stir in the gelatin mixture and vanilla.

Transfer the mixture to a metal bowl set in a bowl of ice-cold water, and stir it until thickened but not set, about 15 minutes. Fold in the remaining 5 cups of berries, and pour the filling into the crust, spreading the mixture evenly.

Chill the tart, covered loosely, for at least 4 hours, or until it has set, and up to 1 day. Serve it with the whipped cream.

Take It Outdoors

One twist on the progressive dinner theme is the Porch and Patio Dinner, where each home takes up a musical theme for its food, entertainment, and decorations. Held during warmer weather, the party stays outdoors. One summer, the hors d'oeuvres house picked Jimmy Buffett and served Key West–style food, decorated the porch with crepe paper and fans, and had Buffett tunes playing. The second stop was the entrée course, where the musical theme was jazz. The food was New Orleans–style, the decorations were Mardi Gras, and the music—well, you guessed it. The dessert house featured Mozart with delicate pastries.

"COOKIE" CRUST TART

A cross between a pie crust and a shortbread cookie, this very easy pastry is the perfect base for summer fruit tarts. Peaches, plums, or berries would all be good topping choices.

- 1/4 pound (1 stick) unsalted butter, softened
- 1/4 cup confectioners' sugar
- 1/2 teaspoon vanilla extract
- 1 cup all-purpose flour
- 1/2 teaspoon salt
- 1/2 cup chopped pecans
- 2 pints (4 cups) hulled strawberries, other berries, or sliced fruit such as peaches
- 1/2 cup currant jelly

Preheat the oven to 400°F.

Pulse the butter, confectioners' sugar, and vanilla in the food processor until the mixture resembles coarse crumbs. Add the flour, salt, and nuts, and pulse again until well combined.

Pat the dough into a greased 9-inch tart pan. Bake the crust until it is golden, about 10 to 12 minutes, and then cool it on a rack.

When the crust is completely cooled, top it with the fruit of your choice, arranging the pieces attractively. Heat the currant jelly in a small saucepan until liquid; brush the fruit with currant glaze, and allow it to set for 30 minutes before serving.

BETTER THAN PUMPKIN PIE

makes 18 servings

Tastes just like pumpkin pie—but it's so much easier! This recipe comes from a very busy nurse-midwife, and mother of three college kids. Who knew a cake mix could come in so handy! Serve with whipped cream or ice cream.

$2^{1}/_{2}$ cups (28-ounce can) pumpkin puree

2 cups milk

6 large eggs

$1^{1}/_{2}$ cups sugar

1 teaspoon salt

2 teaspoons ground cinnamon

$^{1}/_{2}$ teaspoon ground cloves

1 teaspoon ground ginger

1 (18-ounce) package yellow cake mix

$^{1}/_{4}$ pound (1 stick) butter

$^{1}/_{2}$ cup chopped nuts, optional

Preheat the oven to 350°F.

In a mixer bowl, combine the pumpkin, milk, eggs, sugar, salt, and spices. Beat at medium speed until blended. Pour the mixture into a 9 × 12–inch cake pan.

In a separate bowl, pour the dry cake mix. Cut the butter into the cake mix until it is crumbly (or use a food processor).

Sprinkle the crumb mixture over the pumpkin mixture. Top the crumbs with the chopped nuts, if using.

Bake until the crumbs are golden, about 50 minutes to 1 hour.

Serve this dessert warm or cool.

CHOCOLATE FONDUE WITH FRESH FRUIT

makes 18 servings

Almost everyone has a fondue set lurking in the back of a cupboard. Bring it out for this fun, communal dessert. Use a great store-bought cake, Tobler chocolate, and bursting ripe fruit. Nothing could be finer — or easier!

12 ounces semisweet or bittersweet chocolate, cut into chunks

1 cup heavy cream

$^1/_4$ cup brandy, cherry liquor, or an additional $^1/_4$ cup whipping cream

1 loaf pound cake (16 ounces) cut into 1-inch cubes

1 pineapple, peeled, cored, and cut into cubes

1 pint fresh strawberries, hulled

4 tangerines, peeled and separated into sections

Melt the chocolate in a medium saucepan over very low heat, or in the microwave, being careful not to scorch it. Stir in the whipping cream and brandy until the mixture's well blended and smooth.

Transfer the mixture to a fondue pot or chafing dish. Arrange the cake and fruit around the chocolate mixture, and provide each guest with a long-handled fork for dipping. Dig in!

beyond chip-and-dip

One great reason to gather is to play games. Some parties use a game as an excuse to gather and gab, others gather to have serious fun. I belonged to a neighborhood poker night that got so serious, results were e-mailed out the next day in an Excel spreadsheet. Most neighborhood game nights are either for all men or all women. Some people object to that, but I think it's great. Letting your guard down and having an honest conversation can be tough when it's couples, or if kids are running around. What is important is that it is an open invitation. Serve wine or beer, put out some exotic (or fattening!) munchables, and deal 'em out!

CHEESE LACE

makes 16 servings as an appetizer

Like potato chips, but better! Bunco ladies love 'em!

8 ounces Monterey Jack cheese, cut into
$^1/_2 \times ^1/_4$–inch cubes

Preheat the oven to 350°F. Spray one or two baking sheets with vegetable cooking spray. Arrange the cheese squares on the baking sheet, allowing 2 inches of border around the edges and between each square.

Bake until the cheese is melted and bubbly, about 7 minutes. Let the cheese cool on the baking sheet until just set, about 2 minutes; then use a metal spatula to transfer it to a wire rack to cool and harden.

Serve these appetizers at room temperature. They can be stored in an airtight container for up to 2 days.

easy chicken
empanadas

EASY CHICKEN EMPANADAS

makes 16 empanadas

Empanadas travel well; so make them in the afternoon, and then carry them in a cloth-lined basket to your poker night. Refrigerator biscuits cut down the time on this tasty snack.

$^1/_3$	cup raisins
$^1/_2$	cup boiling water
$^2/_3$	cup minced onion
3	tablespoons vegetable oil
1	pound finely diced raw chicken (about 2 large boneless, skinless breast halves)
3	tablespoons toasted pine nuts
3	tablespoons chopped stuffed green olives
$1^1/_4$	teaspoons salt
$^3/_4$	teaspoon ground cumin
$^1/_2$	teaspoon crushed red pepper
	Pinch of cinnamon
3	tubes refrigerator biscuits
1	large egg, beaten

In a small bowl, combine the raisins and boiling water. Set them aside to soften.

In a large skillet, cook the onion in oil over medium heat until softened but not browned. Stir in the chicken, pine nuts, olives, salt, cumin, red pepper, cinnamon, and drained raisins. Cook, stirring often, until the chicken is cooked through and no longer pink, about 5 minutes. Remove the filling from the heat, and let it cool.

Preheat the oven to 350°F. Roll or flatten each biscuit to about 3 inches and about ⅛ inch thick. Divide the filling among the rounds, using about 2 teaspoons for each. Brush the edges with water. Fold the rounds in half, into crescents, and crimp the edges with a fork to seal them.

Arrange the empanadas on a greased baking sheet, and brush them with the beaten egg. Bake until the packets are golden, about 30 minutes.

Mainly Men

Andrew Wertheim recently became part of a Friday night men's gathering affectionately called the Cave because one frequent venue was a basement. It's an informal, standing invitation: Join the Cave, and spend an evening with the guys in the neighborhood. Some nights only three men show up, and some nights there are seven or eight.

Usually the evening includes a movie, the only criterion for which is that it must be a bad movie. (Past screenings have included *Dirty Dancing* and *Ishtar*.) Andrew recently took a turn hosting, and his theme for the evening was Russian Cave. He'd brought back Russian vodka from a trip abroad, and that, along with some caviar, gave the weekly gathering a fun twist.

PIZZA BITES

pizza
bites

makes 12 servings

Pack along a plastic container of these super-easy snacks to feed the hordes of hungry bowlers at your next bowling night; they're best at room temperature.

2 cups shredded Cheddar cheese

1 (8-ounce) can tomato sauce

$\frac{1}{3}$ cup extra virgin olive oil

1 (6-ounce) can chopped ripe olives

1 (6-ounce) can chopped green chiles

$\frac{1}{4}$ cup chopped scallions

2 garlic cloves, minced (1 teaspoon)

$\frac{1}{4}$ teaspoon salt

$1\frac{1}{2}$ teaspoons crushed red pepper flakes

6 English muffins, split

In a medium bowl, combine the Cheddar, tomato sauce, olive oil, chopped olives, chiles, scallions, garlic, salt, and red pepper. Blend until the ingredients are well mixed. (This mixture may be refrigerated, covered, for up to 3 days.)

Preheat the oven to 400°F. Place the English muffins cut side up on a baking sheet. Spread a scant ¼ cup of the cheese mixture over each muffin half.

Bake the pizza bites for 10 to 15 minutes, until the cheese is melted and the muffins are lightly toasted.

Cut each half into quarters, and serve them hot.

POTTED PECAN SHRIMP

makes 2 cups

This dish is great to carry when the party is not at your house. Just remember to put your name on the bottom of the crock so you'll get it back.

1 (8-ounce) package cream cheese, softened

2 tablespoons finely chopped celery

2 tablespoons beer

2 teaspoons grated onion

$1/4$ teaspoon Worcestershire sauce

$1/8$ teaspoon dry mustard

$1/2$ cup cooked chopped shelled shrimp

$1/2$ cup chopped pecans, toasted at 350°F for 5 to 7 minutes

In a medium bowl, combine the cream cheese, celery, beer, onion, Worcestershire, and mustard. Blend well.

Stir in the shrimp and toasted pecans. Pack the mixture into a crock or other serving container, and cover and refrigerate it for at least 1 hour and no more than 2 days. Serve this dish with crackers.

CHICKEN LIVER MASH

Whether you grew up on Grandma's chopped liver or crostini Toscana, this rich, savory spread is comfort food at its best. Always welcome on poker night!

1 pound trimmed chicken livers

$^1/_4$ pound (1 stick) butter or $^1/_2$ cup rendered chicken fat

2 finely chopped medium yellow onions

4 chopped hard-boiled eggs

1 teaspoon salt

$^1/_2$ teaspoon freshly ground pepper

Crackers, matzos, or rye, for serving

Rinse the livers under cold water, and pat them dry.

Melt 4 tablespoons of the butter in a large frying pan. Cook the livers over medium-high heat until they're nicely browned outside, but still pink inside, about 5 minutes. Remove the livers with a slotted spoon and set them aside in a mixing bowl.

In the same pan, melt the remaining butter. Add the onions, reduce the heat to medium-low, and cook until they are golden, 5 to 7 minutes. Add the cooked onions to the bowl with the chicken livers, scraping any pan juices into the bowl.

Add the hard-boiled eggs, salt, and pepper to the bowl, and mash the mixture with a fork until well blended. Serve Chicken Liver Mash immediately with crackers, or cover and refrigerate it for up to 2 days.

WARM PIZZA DIP

warm pizza dip

makes 4 cups

Who says you can't make a meal of this?

8 ounces cream cheese, softened

1 cup pizza sauce

1/2 cup chopped scallions

8 ounces shredded mozzarella cheese

1 (3-ounce) package sliced pepperoni, coarsely chopped

1 (3-ounce) can sliced ripe olives

1 teaspoon dry Italian seasoning

Preheat the oven to 350°F.

Spread the cream cheese over the bottom of a greased 9-inch round baking dish. Top it with the pizza sauce, scallions, cheese, pepperoni, and olives. Sprinkle the top with Italian seasoning.

Bake the dip for about 20 minutes. Serve it warm with crackers, crostini, or sliced baguettes.

poker night

Scratch the image of blue cigar smoke, beer cans, and men in T-shirts huddled around a cluttered card table. Instead, picture twenty or so women sipping wine at three tables, poring over the rules for Midnight Baseball. Our Indian Village Poker Night started out with a handful of women and has now grown to a neighborhood event that players attend as they can.

To get started you need a few boxes of poker chips, several decks of cards, some written instructions (see page 127–129), and the willingness to concede that the first few hands will be very dumb. At first we were all consulting the cheat sheet to determine if three of a kind beat a full house, but very quickly the players figured it out, and it was loads of fun. Watching women decide how much to bet is great entertainment; so many of us spend all day figuring out how to save a few pennies, blowing it on a card hand is hard. Even tougher for some is the bluffing part.

Like bunco parties, the card games begin later so young kids can be sent off to bed. This group plays every other Wednesday night and has a sign-up sheet for hosting duty. The host usually supplies the nibble food along with wine and beer. Each year the group has an end-of-year party to celebrate the top winner and hand out gag prizes.

poker rules and cheat sheet

Here are the poker rules and some of the poker hands from the Official Indian Village Poker cheat sheet and several other card games.

winning hands, best to worst

Five of a Kind	
Royal Flush	10, Jack, Queen, King, Ace, all of the same suit
Straight Flush	Five cards in numerical order, all of the same suit
Four of a Kind	
Full House	Three of a kind plus a pair
Flush	Any five cards of the same suit
Straight	Five cards in numerical order, any suit
Three of a Kind	
Two Pair	
One Pair	
High Card	
(Best low hand:	Ace, 2, 3, 4, 6)

house rules

- White chips are 10 cents; red chips are 25 cents; and blue chips are 50 cents.
- The maximum bet is $1.50.
- Three raises per person are allowed per betting round.
- Ante is 10 cents, unless otherwise called by dealer—dealer must ante twice.
- Double Ace flushes (only double and only Aces) are possible with wild cards.
- In the event of a showdown with wild cards and naturals, the natural hand wins over the wild-card hand *only* if the rest of the hand is the same; that is, a wild, Ace, King, 9, 5 will beat Ace, Ace, Queen, 9, 5, but will lose to Ace, Ace, King, 9, 5.
- If all cards are dealt facedown, the player left of the dealer opens; with cards dealt up, the highest hand showing opens.

{continued from poker rules and cheat sheet}

- Betting goes clockwise.

- Out-of-turn betting is penalized—25 cents to the pot.

- If you fold, do so when it is your turn to bet, and place all cards facedown.

- If you call your hand too low, you have to stick with what you called.

- The dealer of the previous round prepares the deck after her deal.

- You do not need to show your Ace in draw.

- Unless otherwise stated, in all games with widows you can use any number of cards from the widow.

- In low poker, Ace is either high or low, but a straight is a high hand.

- For low poker, at declaration, 0 chips is low; 1 chip is high; 2 chips is both. *If you declare both, you must win both;* if anyone declares both high and low and loses on either, she automatically loses all, even if she won the other. (If she won the other pot, then the one to whom she lost also loses, and the whole pot goes to the one who did win.)

rules of the game(s)

Here are the rules for the classic poker games and a few fun variations.

5-CARD STUD

- The deal is 1 card down, 4 cards up (or all 5 down).

- Betting round begins after the first up cards are dealt; then a bet is made for every new card thereafter.

- The dealer can call wild cards before the deal only.

7-CARD STUD

- The deal is 2 cards down, 4 cards up, 1 card down.

- Betting round begins after the first up cards are dealt, then at every new card thereafter.

- The dealer can call wild cards before the deal only.

5- (OR 7-) CARD DRAW

- The deal is 5 (or 7) cards down.

- One betting round, and then everyone can exchange up to three cards (four if you have an Ace), and then another betting round.

- The dealer can call wild cards or minimum hand to open before the deal.

NIGHTTIME BASEBALL

- The deal is 7 cards, all facedown.

- No one looks at her cards.

- The first player begins to turn cards over; the second player turns cards over until she has beaten the first player's hand, and so forth. Every player must bet (or pass) each time a card is turned.

- 3s and 9s are wild.
- If you turn over a 4, you can buy any faceup card for 25 cents.

FOLLOW THE QUEEN

- The deal is 2 cards down, 4 cards up, 1 card down.
- Betting round begins after the first up cards are dealt; then at every new card thereafter.
- Queens are wild; the up card after the queen is also wild, but note—the wild up card after the queen can change. If the last up card is a queen, only the queen is wild.

DAYTIME BASEBALL

- The deal is 2 cards down, 4 cards up, 1 card down.
- Betting round begins after the first up cards are dealt; then at every new card thereafter.
- 3s and 9s are wild.
- If you are dealt a faceup 3, you must either match the pot or fold.
- If you are dealt a faceup 4, you can buy any faceup card for 25 cents.

PIG IN POKE

- The deal is 4 cards down, then later 1 card down.
- One betting round; then the dealer places one card faceup in the middle, which determines the wild card (the card itself isn't played); then another betting round. Then fifth card is dealt, and there's another betting round.

GUTS

- The deal is 3 cards down.
- Each player, simultaneously, either holds his hand or drops all his cards.
- The winner gets the pot—losers each match the pot.
- Keep playing until only one person is holding cards. (But if only one holds or all keep folding in the first 3 games, keep playing.)
- The order of winning hands is 3 of a kind, 3 flush, 3 straight, pair, high card. All else is ignored.

DOUBLE-BARRELED SHOTGUN

- The deal is 3 cards down, then 2 cards down.
- After 3 cards are dealt down, there's a betting round; 1 down and a betting round; 1 down and a betting round; then there's a draw.
- Each player flips a card, and then there's betting round; then another card is flipped, and a betting round.

FRIED POTATO SHELLS

Here's an easy hors d'oeuvre you can dress up or down with homey or haute toppings. For easy preparation, bake it the day before.

12 small red potatoes, 1 1/2 to 2 inches each

2 to 4 cups peanut or corn oil, for frying

1/2 cup sour cream

garnishes (choose 1 or more, as desired)

Salsa with chopped cilantro or parsley

Crumbled crisp bacon with minced scallions

Chopped black olives

Chopped pimiento-stuffed olives

Finely grated cheese

Caviar

Avocado mashed with lemon and salt

Fresh dill and chives

Preheat oven to 400°F. Pierce the potatoes with a fork, and bake for 40 minutes. Cool the potatoes.

Slice the potatoes in half. Take a small sliver off each potato half, so it will stand without rolling over. Use a melon baller or small spoon to scoop out the center of each potato half, leaving a 1/4-inch shell.

Heat the oil in a heavy pan or wok to 360°F. Cook the potato shells in small batches until they're just browned, about 1 to 2 minutes. Invert them on paper towels to drain them. (The potato shells can be cooled and stored, covered, in the refrigerator, for up to a day.)

Shortly before serving, preheat the oven to 400°F. Fill each potato cavity with 2 teaspoons of sour cream and arrange on a cookie sheet. Bake for about 10 minutes. Top them with a desired garnish, and serve warm.

CHEESE PILLOWS

makes 24 servings as an appetizer

Want to be ready for the holidays? Make these pungent pillows ahead, and freeze them until party time. Then pop them in the oven to bake while you mix the drinks!

1 unsliced white sandwich loaf

2 cups shredded sharp Cheddar cheese

1 cup heavy cream

1 stick softened butter

$^1/_4$ teaspoon cayenne pepper, or to taste

Partially freeze the bread until it is quite firm, about 1 hour. Slice off the crusts, and cut the bread into 1½-inch cubes.

Combine the cheese, cream, butter, and cayenne in a double boiler, and heat over simmering water. Stir until the cheese and butter are melted and blended, about 5 minutes.

Spear individual cubes of bread, and swirl in the warm cheese mixture until each cube is thoroughly coated.

Place the coated cubes on a baking sheet lined with waxed paper. Freeze the cubes for about 1 hour. The cheese cubes are now ready to be stored in heavy plastic bags in the freezer for up to 2 months. Shortly before serving, preheat the oven to 450°F. Arrange the frozen cubes on a baking sheet, and bake them for 5 to 10 minutes, until they're heated and beginning to brown. Serve Cheese Pillows hot with toothpicks.

SMOKED OYSTER DIP

No one will guess this suave blend was easily assembled from convenience foods!

1 (8-ounce) package cream cheese, softened

2 tablespoons mayonnaise

1 teaspoon fresh lemon juice

1/4 teaspoon garlic salt

Dash of Tabasco or other hot sauce

1/2 cup chopped black olives

1 (9-ounce) can smoked oysters, drained and chopped

Crackers, for serving

In a medium bowl, combine the cream cheese, mayonnaise, lemon juice, garlic salt, and Tabasco. Mix them thoroughly. Fold in the olives and smoked oysters.

Transfer the dip to a serving bowl. Cover and refrigerate it for up to 3 days. Serve Smoked Oyster Dip with crackers.

CRAB-AND-JALAPEÑO DIP

dip

makes 3 cups

Put a little zip on the table with this delicious appetizer.

1½ teaspoons olive oil

½ red bell pepper, seeded and diced

1 (14-ounce) can artichoke hearts, diced

1 cup mayonnaise

½ cup grated Parmesan cheese

¼ cup thinly sliced scallions

1 tablespoon Worcestershire sauce

1 tablespoon chopped jalapeño pepper

1½ teaspoons fresh lemon juice

½ teaspoon celery salt

8 ounces crabmeat, picked over for bits of shell

(⅓ cup slivered almonds)

Preheat the oven to 375°F.

Heat the olive oil over medium-high heat. Add the red pepper, and sauté until it is light brown.

Transfer the pepper to a large bowl. Add the artichokes, mayonnaise, Parmesan, scallions, Worcestershire, jalapeño, lemon juice, and celery salt, and stir to combine.

Gently mix in the crab. Transfer the mixture to an 8-inch pie pan. Sprinkle the dip with the almonds, and bake until it's bubbly, about 30 minutes.

Serve this dip with crostini, crackers, or crudités.

very good

bunco parties
what they are and how to get started

Bunco is a simple dice game that allows lots of people to participate. It's usually an all-women night out because, as my sister-in-law, Kirsten, put it, "It's no fun when it's coed, because the guys only play to win!" In her neighborhood, they play about once every other month, rarely in the summer, and she said it was the very best way for her to meet her neighbors. Bunco parties are popular in many parts of the country—it might be just the thing for your neck of the woods.

The game itself is played at tables of four, with six rounds of dice rolling in each set. Players change partners at the end of each round so they get to meet and talk with different people during the evening. It's a breeze to learn, and it is a great icebreaker for new neighbors who may not feel comfortable starting conversations.

The food is all potluck with the host providing sodas and beer or wine. (If you prefer one or the other, bring your own.) To make certain the host has no extra work, the rule is clear: walk in with a platter; leave with a platter. No leftovers or cleanup allowed.

If you think bunco is something you'd like to try, there are plenty of websites with the rules and full explanation of how to play. One that I like is www.buncogame.com.

COCOMIA COOKIES

The first time my sister-in-law, Kirsten, brought these cookies to her local bunco party, she was told she *must* bring them *every* time—they are that good.

2 cups all-purpose flour

$^1/_2$ teaspoon baking soda

$^1/_4$ teaspoon salt

$^3/_4$ cup packed brown sugar

$^1/_2$ cup granulated sugar

$^1/_4$ pound plus 4 tablespoons (1$^1/_2$ sticks) salted butter, softened

2 large eggs

2 teaspoons vanilla extract

6 ounces shredded, unsweetened coconut (about 1 cup)

7 ounces whole macadamia nuts (about 1$^1/_2$ cups)

Preheat the oven to 300°F.

In a medium bowl, combine the flour, soda, and salt. Mix the ingredients well with a wire whisk.

In a large mixer bowl, blend the sugars, and mix at medium speed. Add the butter, and mix to form a grainy paste. Scrape down the sides of the bowl; then add the eggs and vanilla. Beat at medium speed until the mixture is light and fluffy. Add the flour mixture, the coconut, and the macadamia nuts to the sugar mixture, and blend at low speed just until combined. Do not overmix.

Drop the batter by rounded tablespoons onto ungreased cookie sheets, 2 inches apart. Bake for 22 to 24 minutes. Immediately transfer the cookies with a spatula to a cool, flat surface.

go bowling

Is there a bowling alley in your town that you've never set foot in? Try it. My friend Corrine Wagner and her neighbors are not only incredibly creative, but also highly organized. Their potluck bowling party maximizes the number of people that can participate and the amount of fun to be had. Their town boasts an intimate, ten-lane bowling alley that can be rented out on Friday nights, but regardless of the size of the facility in your area, a bowling party can still work. Here's how Corrine and her neighbors did theirs:

+ Four hosts invited four couples each, for a total of twenty couples.

+ Each hosting couple contributed fifty dollars, which covered the rental of the facilities and all the lanes for two and a half hours.

+ Each host was responsible for a task: invitations, RSVPs, rules of the game, and creating scoring cards printed on folded paper to be set at each lane. They also secured a large erasable board, and once they had a sense of who was coming, they listed each couple on the board and created a series of grids to reflect five rounds of play. One of the hosts also was in charge of coming up with cute, inexpensive prizes and categories. Prize categories included Big Balls, the King and Queen Pins, Best Form, and the Gutter Lovers.

Couples were asked to BYOB and to provide a substantial appetizer; in your community, the facility may require you to purchase refreshments on the premises, in which case, it should be a cash bar.

the game

+ The couples fill up the lanes as they arrive, two couples per alley.

+ Each team bowls four frames (two for each player) and totals its score. The score for all four frames goes up on the big scoreboard.

+ The winning couple remains at the same lane. The losers advance one alley to the right.

+ Teams continue bowling and rotating for an hour and a half of play, at which point the game in play is finished up, and scores are recorded. Usually you will fit five to six rounds in.

scoring

As in any bowling game, you get a point for each pin knocked down. Candlepin bowling allows three rolls of the ball per frame; ten-pin bowling allows two. The total number of pins knocked down is the score for that frame.

Strike — all pins are knocked down on the first roll. score, add ten bonus points to the number of pins knocked down on the next two rolls from the next frame.

Spare — knock down all the pins on the second ball, and add ten bonus points to the next roll in the next frame.

According to Corrine, "Everyone had a ball! Queen and King Pins got hand-painted T-shirts that were pretty tacky, but the Big Balls trophy was fought over!"

late-night gathering

Sometimes the best excuse for a party is something as simple as a flower. A close friend told me her grandmother used to have a regular neighborhood gathering when her night-blooming cereus plant blossomed. This exotic flower has a heady fragrance, and is in peak bloom only one night per year. Each year, when the plant had several buds that were ready to open, she would put a sign on the front lawn welcoming neighbors for the big event. They would show up as it got dark, her grandma would serve sherry and cookies, and they would stand around and sniff the blossom and marvel at this touch of the tropics in suburban New Jersey.

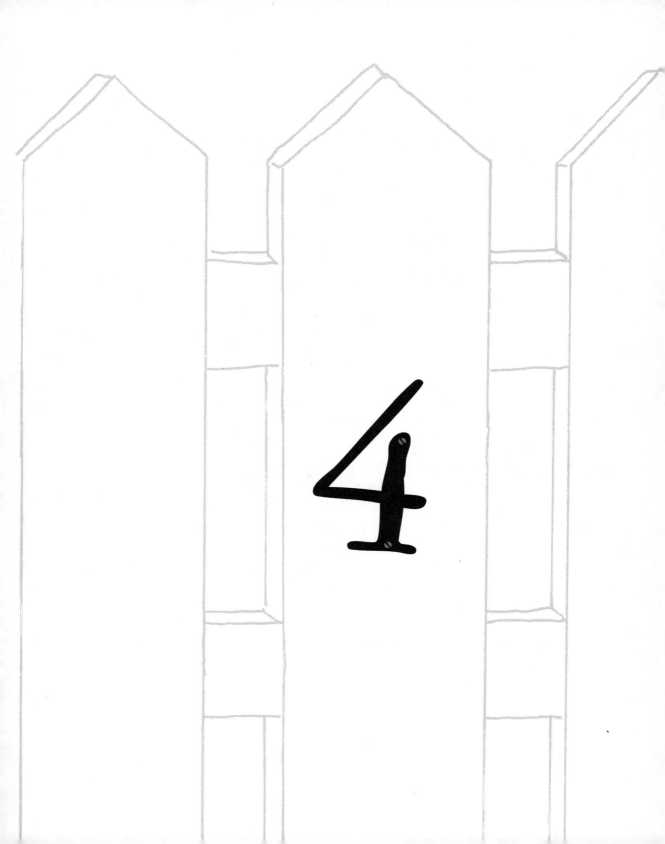

seasons in the neighborhood

Some of the best times in a neighborhood are associated with a seasonal milestone: the start of summer, fall foliage, the winter holidays, or the spring thaw. Each season offers an opportunity for conversation, help, and fun. There are plenty of delicious food ideas, recipes, and specialty drinks that can accompany all the great times. For each season I've described some parties that have been big hits over the years and I've added some other seasonal events, simple ideas that may be just the ticket for your particular community.

spring ♦ Spring just seems to put people in a great mood — especially if your area has long, cold winters. Spring is always about starting over, breaking loose. If a local park, tennis court, playground, or beach could benefit from a few hours of sprucing up, consider throwing a Cleanup party. Two parties made for spring are a Kentucky Derby party and an Easter Sunday egg hunt.

EGG AND SAUSAGE CASSEROLE

makes 12 servings

This really is a meal in one, and who doesn't love breakfast sausage?

2$^1/_4$ cups milk

10 large eggs

1$^1/_2$ teaspoons dry mustard

$^1/_2$ teaspoon salt

4$^1/_2$ cups shredded Cheddar cheese

5 slices white bread (crusts trimmed), cubed

1 pound pork sausage, browned and drained

Preheat the oven to 350°F.

Combine the milk, eggs, mustard, and salt in a mixer bowl. Beat for 1 minute at medium speed or with a whisk. Stir in the cheese, bread, and sausage.

Pour the mixture into an ungreased 9 × 13–inch pan. Bake until a knife inserted into the center comes out clean, about 40 minutes. Cool the casserole for a few moments on a rack, then cut it into squares, and serve.

mexican egg
casserole

DIANE DUFALT'S MEXICAN EGG CASSEROLE

makes 8 to 10 servings

This has been a feature at the Scituate Easter Egg Hunt for years.

6 large eggs, beaten

6 cups (24 ounces) creamy small-curd cottage cheese

³/₄ cup (about 18) finely crushed Ritz crackers

1 (4-ounce) can mild chopped green chiles

³/₄ cup shredded Cheddar cheese

³/₄ cup shredded Monterey Jack cheese

Prepared tomato salsa, for serving

Sour cream, for serving

Preheat the oven to 350°F. Butter a 9 × 12–inch baking dish.

Combine the eggs, cottage cheese, crackers, and chiles in a medium bowl. Combine the Cheddar and Jack cheeses and stir half into the egg mixture. Pour into the prepared pan. Sprinkle the remaining shredded cheeses evenly over the top of the casserole.

Bake the casserole until it is set, about 45 minutes. Let it stand for 5 minutes before cutting it into squares and serving. Let guests help themselves to your favorite salsa and sour cream.

BAKED STUFFED FRENCH TOAST

makes 8 to 10 servings

Stuff the bread slices and soak them in the egg mixture overnight for the fluffiest, most golden French toasts.

> 1 pint strawberries, hulled and sliced
>
> 2 teaspoons sugar
>
> 1 large loaf challah or Italian country bread (a wide, long loaf)
>
> 8 ounces cream cheese, cut into 8 to 10 slices
>
> 8 eggs
>
> 1½ cups milk
>
> 1 teaspoon almond extract, optional
>
> 2 tablespoons vegetable oil
>
> Maple syrup, for serving

Toss the strawberry slices with the sugar in a small bowl. Cut the bread loaf into 8 to 10 1½-inch-thick slices and cut a wide pocket into the side of each slice. Insert a piece of cream cheese into each pocket, then a few slices of strawberries. Arrange the stuffed slices on a jelly roll pan in a single layer. Mix together the eggs, milk, and almond extract and pour over the bread, soaking each slice; cover and refrigerate for up to 12 hours.

Preheat the oven to 350°F. Heat 2 teaspoons of the oil in a skillet and when it's hot, add 2 or 3 bread slices and lightly brown on both sides. Transfer to a baking sheet and fry the remaining slices the same way. When all are browned, bake the slices for 15 to 20 minutes until puffed.

Serve hot with the remaining strawberries and syrup.

let the hunt begin

I had never thought of an egg hunt as a neighborhood-wide activity until I talked to Scituate, Massachusetts, resident Brenda Sportack, who has turned a quaint, old-fashioned game into an art form and a tradition that truly is special.

As with so many local traditions, this one had humble beginnings. Brenda went to a neighbor's Easter egg hunt with five other families and her two-year-old daughter to hunt for dyed hard-boiled eggs. Today, Brenda plays host to sixty-five families, supplying a ribbon-cutting ceremony, hand-painted eggs, and fabulous food for all. "I can't quit now," Brenda says. "My kids start talking about it months in advance. They'd be devastated."

For more than eleven years, Brenda's Egg Hunt has become the place to be on Easter Sunday. "My yard is so colorful that morning, you drive by and can't believe it," she says. Brenda's unique touch was to make an egg for every person attending, putting a name and the year on each one. When the event had grown to the point that she was hard-boiling 144 eggs—starting several weeks before the event—she knew a change was in order. No way could anyone eat those eggs that had been sitting out for weeks. The following year Brenda bought dozens of wooden eggs with a small flat bottom and hand-painted each one. On the bottom she wrote a family's name and the year. Brenda swears she's not an artist, "And I don't pretend to be." Nonetheless, they are coveted souvenirs of a treasured family activity, and many families have accumulated quite a collection.

Families know the hunt begins at 10:45 A.M. sharp, and despite other obligations, every family makes room in their day for the hunt, the food, and the company. In addition to the egg hunt, Brenda and the neighbors pull together a potluck brunch menu with its own traditions. Over the years the assignments have become standard. (With 250 people, it takes real planning.) Some people bring grilled lamb, marinated shrimp, or wonderful casseroles. In the beginning many brought baked goods, but the kids all wanted doughnuts, so today there are store-bought doughnuts for the kids who want them and entrées and salads for everyone else. One neighbor carves a watermelon into an ornate bunny basket and fills it with a terrific fruit salad. Brenda cooks two different egg casseroles on the morning of the party, one a sausage-and-cheese dish, the other Southwestern inspired. In addition to her double recipe, several neighbors pitch in and make the same. For beverages,

Brenda sets out regular and decaf coffee, orange juice, and champagne. (She used to mix the OJ and champagne in a punch bowl for mimosas, but a child drank from the wrong bowl once too often!)

Over the years of hosting her annual egg hunt, Brenda Sportack has found returning the serving dishes from potluck offerings has been a problem. "I have quite a collection of unclaimed dishes!" Brenda says. She plans to set up a table covered in orphaned dishes this year in hopes that their owners will reclaim them.

The hunt itself has evolved, and the ritual is clear. A four-inch-wide pastel ribbon is strung across the porch stairs that lead to the backyard. Brenda selects a family to cut the ribbon, usually a family that has just welcomed a new baby. Once the ribbon is cut, the kids of all ages rush into the yard to find the egg with their name on it. Toddlers count on the older kids to help locate their eggs. In addition to the hand-painted wooden egg with the family name, each child looks for two plastic eggs with their own name. Inside are trinkets or, for the older kids, a raffle ticket. Brenda conducts the raffle right after the hunt, and it includes items like a makeup kit or gift certificate. But the hand-painted wooden eggs are the most highly prized.

Here is Brenda Sportack's method for painting wooden eggs. She allows about six weeks to create all sixty-five she prepares annually.

Step One: Each egg is painted with several coats of acrylic paint. Brenda uses old egg cartons to prop them up, painting first the tops, letting them dry, and then painting the bottoms.

Step Two: Each egg is painted with an acrylic varnish. Brenda recommends a quick-drying one because the bottom is painted and set to dry before doing the top. Use a good half-inch brush. This step is important because it makes the surface easier to decorate.

Step Three: Decorate each egg using acrylic paint pens. These pens come in lots of colors and run about four dollars each. Brenda uses three or four different colors on each egg, making floral designs on some and geometric designs on others. If you like, use a pencil to draw lightly on the egg and divide it into sections to make sure the design comes out even.

Step Four: When the design is dry, each egg gets two coats of varnish.

COUNTRY ITALIAN
BREAKFAST CASSEROLE

makes 6 servings

Want to get ready the night before? Here's a tasty dish. This really takes the standard egg casserole to a new level, but it's just as easy. It doubles beautifully.

1 cup milk

1/2 cup dry white wine

1 day-old loaf French bread, cut into 1/2-inch slices

8 ounces prosciutto, thinly sliced

2 cups arugula (1 bunch)

3 tablespoons extra virgin olive oil

1 pound herb-flavored goat cheese, crumbled

3 ripe tomatoes, sliced

1/2 cup prepared basil pesto

4 large eggs, beaten

Salt and freshly ground pepper, to taste

1/2 cup heavy cream

One day before serving, mix the milk and wine in a shallow bowl. Dip 1 or 2 slices of bread in the milk mixture. Gently squeeze as much liquid as possible from the bread without tearing it.

Place the bread in a lightly greased 12-inch round or oval baking dish, and cover it with a slice of prosciutto, several arugula leaves dipped in olive oil, several blobs of goat cheese, and a few tomato slices. Dot sparingly with the pesto. Repeat the process with the remaining ingredients, overlapping the bread slices slightly, until the dish is filled.

Beat the eggs with the salt and pepper to taste, and pour them evenly over the layers. Cover the casserole with plastic wrap, and refrigerate it overnight.

The following day, remove the dish from the refrigerator, and let it warm to room temperature. Preheat the oven to 350°F.

Drizzle the casserole with cream, and bake until it is puffed and brown, 45 minutes to 1 hour. Serve immediately.

Spruce Up

Each spring one neighborhood does more than just tend to public areas. Each year they select one or two projects that involve a neighbor's property. Someone may need a tree limb cut or a fence rebuilt. The notice goes out with the day, the time, and the projects. Everyone who is able to help does so. It all ends with a casual lunch served potluck style. It's not a barn raising, but it sure has a lot of the same feel.

let the race begin

My husband and I give a Kentucky Derby party every year. The race takes place on the first Saturday in May, and for me, it is how spring begins. I decorate with fresh-cut apple blossoms and early spring greens, load my table with salads and sliced meats, and invite the entire neighborhood.

If you're nervous about asking folks to your home, this is a great first party to throw, because people don't have to commit to a whole evening, and the betting gives everyone something to talk about. Whenever we've given this party, we have invited every single neighbor that we have met, even if we've only waved on the street. When neighbors open their mail and see the illustration of a horse dancing on its hind legs (see opposite) that adorned our invite for the last ten years, they know immediately that the Allens are doing their Derby party again. The wording is simple: "You are cordially invited to the Allen Clubhouse for the one hundred and twenty-eighth running of the Kentucky Derby." We let them know when the betting window opens (the start of the party) and post time, which is usually 6:04 P.M. EST.

My mother always said that if you're going to serve alcohol, you've got to serve protein. With mint juleps and a full bar, I try to provide a full meal. I have hors d'oeuvres set out when guests arrive. Just as the race is getting under way, I put out all kinds of salads and sliced meats. Paper plates and plastic forks (no knives) keep cleanup simple, but I do try to make the presentation special with a good white linen tablecloth, fresh flowers, and colorful paper napkins. The evening ends with dessert, set on a series of trays, and coffee on the buffet.

Part of the fun of this party is enabling the guests to bet on the actual race. We put up big posters that list the horses, how they've done recently, and the morning odds. (We also pick up *The Racing Form* so serious bettors can get more extensive background on each horse.)

The week of the party we make betting slips with the name of each horse and the kind of bet that can be made. Four betting slips fit on one 8½ × 11–inch page, and we print a quantity in two different colors. We staple a full sheet of carbon paper between a sheet of each color, giving us four slips, each with a carbon slip and a duplicate. We use an Excel spreadsheet program to keep track of the bets for win, place, and show. Our guests just have to hand in their slip; we enter the information.

The betting slips and horse selection gives everyone instant conversation, and it makes it so much livelier than standing around, drink in hand, without a clue what to say in a room full of strangers. Comparing your betting choices is a great icebreaker. The pool of money grows quickly with lots of last-minute bets getting placed. (We decided early on that guests who couldn't make it to the party weren't allowed to phone in any bets.) Since the pot of money is divided up only among guests with winning tickets, everyone starts trying to figure out who is betting on what horse to see if there might be a horse that few have placed bets on but still might win.

Moments before the race, the guests crowd around the four TVs we hook up around the first floor. Cheers turn into screams as those holding winning tickets begin jumping, waving their tickets, or smiling smugly. One year, a single person walked away with five hundred dollars.

I start cooking early in the week—salad dressings first and then hors d'oeuvres. Over the years, I've settled on some favorite recipes for a Saturday afternoon crowd.

CORRINE'S SUN-DRIED SPREAD

makes 2 cups

My friend Corrine shared this tasty spread recipe years ago. Everyone in her neighborhood and mine loves it.

1 (3-ounce) jar sun-dried tomatoes in oil

1 small onion, finely chopped

3 garlic cloves, minced (1½ teaspoons)

2 teaspoons capers

1 teaspoon sugar

Salt and freshly ground black pepper to taste

1 baguette, cut into ⅓-inch slices

Extra virgin olive oil, for brushing

3 ounces garlic-and-herb-flavored cheese

Drain the oil from the tomatoes into a skillet, and warm it over medium-high heat. Add the onion and garlic, and sauté until they're softened, 5 or 6 minutes. Cut the tomatoes into julienne strips. Drain the oil from the skillet, and add the tomatoes. Simmer for 2 minutes. Add the capers, sugar, and salt and pepper, and heat through. Brush the baguette slices with a little olive oil, arrange them on a cookie sheet, and bake until they're lightly toasted.

Spread each toasted bread slice with some cheese, and top it with some of the sun-dried-tomato mixture. Serve at once.

SMOKY SALMON LOG

makes 3 1/2 cups

An assortment of good-quality crackers or crostini make an able backer for these smoky pink rounds.

 1 (16-ounce) can red salmon

 1 (8-ounce) package cream cheese, softened

 1 tablespoon fresh lemon juice

 2 teaspoons minced onion

 1 teaspoon prepared white horseradish

 1/2 teaspoon Liquid Smoke, or to taste

 1/4 teaspoon salt

 1/3 cup chopped pecans or almonds

 3 tablespoons chopped dried dill

Drain the salmon, and discard any bones; then flake the meat with a fork. In a medium bowl, combine the cream cheese, lemon juice, onion, horseradish, Liquid Smoke, and salt, and blend well. Mix in the flaked salmon and form the mixture into a log.

Wrap the log in plastic, and refrigerate it until it's firm, at least 1 hour.

Just before serving, combine the chopped nuts and dill, and mix them well. Roll the log in the nut mixture, coating it.

QUICK CRAB MOUSSE

You'll never believe you can make a half pound of crab feed a crowd! Sliced on a glass plate and surrounded by crackers or cucumber rounds, it looks quite lovely. You can also serve slices on individual plates for a ladylike luncheon dish.

1 envelope unflavored gelatin

2 (10^1/$_2$-ounce) cans condensed cream of mushroom soup

1 (8-ounce) package cream cheese, softened

^{1}/$_2$ cup mayonnaise

^{1}/$_2$ cup sour cream

1 cup chopped celery

^{1}/$_2$ cup chopped scallions

1 (2-ounce) jar pimiento, drained and diced

^{1}/$_8$ teaspoon salt

1 teaspoon fresh lemon juice

^{1}/$_8$ teaspoon hot pepper sauce

^{1}/$_2$ pound lump crabmeat, picked over for cartilage or shell

^{1}/$_4$ cup chopped fresh parsley

Crackers or bread rounds, for serving

In a small bowl, soften the gelatin in 2 tablespoons of cold water.

In a medium saucepan over medium-low heat, heat the undiluted soup, stirring occasionally, to just under a boil. Stir in the cream cheese, a few tablespoons at a time, whisking until the mixture is well blended, and cook about 3 minutes. Stir in the gelatin mixture, and remove the pan from the heat.

Whisk in the mayonnaise and sour cream. Stir in the celery, scallions, diced pimiento, salt, lemon juice, and hot sauce. Gently fold in the crab and parsley.

Oil a loaf pan or a 6- or 7-cup mold, pour the mixture into it, cover with plastic wrap, and refrigerate until set, about 4 hours or up to 2 days. Unmold the mousse and serve it with crackers.

MINT JULEP

makes 1 large drink

No Derby party is complete without this Kentucky classic. Below is an official recipe, but the amount of mint should be determined by how your guests feel about the taste of bourbon. This drink works just fine with 2 or 3 sprigs.

    8 to 10 mint leaves
    1 teaspoon superfine sugar or 1 sugar cube
    1/2 jigger water
    1 cup crushed ice
    2 1/2 ounces bourbon whiskey

Crush (muddle) the mint leaves in a 10-ounce silver mint julep cup with the sugar and water. Fill the cup with crushed ice.

Add the bourbon, and mix vigorously until the cup is frosted. Fill the cup with more ice, if needed.

Decorate the drink with another sprig of mint. Add a slice of fruit, if desired.

STRAWBERRY SPINACH SALAD WITH MANDARINS AND ALMONDS

makes 10 to 12 cups

Making salad got so much easier when they started selling triple-washed baby spinach and lettuce in cello packs. For the Derby party, I triple all the ingredients.

6 cups rinsed, torn baby spinach

2 cups torn leaf lettuce

1 (22-ounce) can mandarin orange sections, drained

1/2 cup sliced fresh strawberries

3 tablespoons vegetable oil

1 tablespoon fresh lemon juice

1 teaspoon sugar

1/4 teaspoon salt

1/2 cup slivered almonds, toasted

In a large bowl, toss together the spinach, lettuce, orange sections, and strawberries. Cover the salad and chill it for up to 8 hours.

In a jar with a lid, combine the oil, lemon juice, sugar, and salt. Shake the dressing and pour it over the chilled salad. Toss the salad, and sprinkle it with the toasted almonds. Serve at once.

GRILLED VEGETABLE SALAD

makes 16 servings

Add the sweet, smoky flavor of grilling to a summertime salad. You will need shish-kebab rods.

4 Vidalia onions, quartered

4 red bell peppers, quartered and cored

4 green bell peppers, quartered

Extra virgin olive oil, for brushing

4 ripe red tomatoes, seeded and diced

6 ounces goat cheese

Balsamic vinegar

Preheat a gas or charcoal grill. Soak 12 wooden skewers in water for 20 minutes or so. Thread the onion quarters onto the skewers; then skewer the peppers on their own rods. Brush all the vegetables with olive oil.

Grill the onions over low heat for 10 minutes; then add the peppers. Continue grilling, turning over the vegetables regularly, until all are very tender, about 30 minutes. Some charring is fine. Brush the shish kebabs with more oil if necessary.

As soon as the vegetables are cool enough to handle but still warm, chop them into large bite-size pieces and place them in a bowl with the diced tomatoes. Crumble the goat cheese into the bowl, and toss well; the cheese should melt slightly. Sprinkle the salad with balsamic vinegar.

Line a serving platter with graceful greenery and top it with the vegetables. Serve this salad warm or at room temperature.

WALNUT-AND-APPLE WILD RICE SALAD

makes 6 servings

Walnut oil in the dressing really boosts the flavor of this hearty salad. It's best when served right after being made, although it can also be refrigerated for an hour or two. This can be doubled, tripled, or more.

- 1 cup wild rice
- 1 small Granny Smith apple, peeled and coarsely chopped
- 1/3 cup currants
- 1/2 cup chopped walnuts, toasted in preheated 350°F oven until golden
- 1/4 cup red wine vinegar
- 2 tablespoons walnut oil
- 1/3 cup extra virgin olive oil

In a saucepan, combine the wild rice with 4 cups of barely salted water, and bring to a boil. Lower the temperature and simmer until the rice is tender, about 40 minutes. Drain.

In a large serving bowl, combine the cooked rice with the chopped apple, currants, and walnuts, and toss well. Stir together the vinegar and oils in a small bowl. Pour the dressing over the rice, and toss again. Serve this salad immediately.

CHICKEN SALAD WITH RED GRAPES AND PECANS

makes 24 servings

A rich combination of jewel-colored red grapes, crunchy pecans, and grilled chicken flavored with a pungent Roquefort-sherry mayonnaise, this substantial salad has been on my Derby party menu every year, and it's been a hit from day one! It's based on a recipe I discovered in *The Silver Palate Cookbook* and tinkered with over the years. You can grill the chicken a day in advance.

8 whole boneless chicken breasts (16 halves)

4 tablespoons olive oil

2 cups diced celery

3 cups seedless red grapes, halved

1 1/2 cups pecan halves

3 cups Roquefort Dressing (see page 158)

Preheat the grill, or make a charcoal fire. Brush the chicken breasts with the oil, and grill them over medium heat until just done, about 10 minutes per side.

Cut the chicken into 1-inch chunks, and combine it with the celery, grapes, and pecans in a large bowl. Toss the salad with the mayonnaise. You can cover and refrigerate this salad for up to 8 hours.

ROQUEFORT DRESSING

makes about 3 cups

2 large egg yolks

1 tablespoon Dijon mustard

2 tablespoons sherry vinegar

1 1/2 cups vegetable oil

1 cup crumbled Roquefort cheese

Salt and freshly ground black pepper to taste

Process the egg yolks, mustard, and vinegar in a food processor fitted with a steel blade until just combined, about 30 seconds. With the machine running, pour the oil in a thin steady stream through the feed tube to make a thick mayonnaise.

Add the Roquefort, and process until combined but not smooth. Season to taste with salt and pepper. Transfer the mayonnaise to a clean jar, cover it, and refrigerate for up to 1 week.

FIG-AND-DATE CHUTNEY

fig-and-date chutney

makes 5 cups

This a staple of Liza Henshaw's parties, where she serves it to spruce up sliced, grilled pork tenderloin or a store-bought honey-baked ham and small dinner rolls precut for sandwiches.

- 1 pint fresh figs
- 1½ cups chopped dates or dried apricots
- 1 cup sherry, port, or Madeira
- ¼ cup plus 2 tablespoons olive oil
- 12 garlic cloves, unpeeled
- 1 cup minced Vidalia onion
- ¼ teaspoon cayenne pepper
- ½ teaspoon crushed whole cloves
- ½ cup chopped walnuts

Wash and stem the figs. Slice each fig into 6 rings, and then in half. Combine the dates and sherry in a small bowl, and set them aside to steep.

Heat ¼ cup of the oil in a pan. Add the garlic, and cook it slowly over low heat, turning the cloves often. Let the garlic cloves cook; then drain and peel them, reserving the oil for another use.

Sauté the onion in the remaining 2 tablespoons of oil until just caramelized; add the figs, and sauté briefly. Add the sherry and dates, the cayenne, and the cloves and walnuts. Store the chutney refrigerated in a covered jar.

BAKED BRIE IN PHYLLO

makes 40 servings as an appetizer

Every single time I've served this, it evaporates off the buffet table. It's extremely adaptable, too. A friend made it with raspberry preserves, but you can use your imagination. How about filling the cheese with roasted red peppers? Or pesto? Anything goes! You can assemble the Brie early in the day and bake it just before serving time.

1 (2.2-pound) wheel Brie
(about 8 inches in diameter)

$^1/_3$ cup loosely packed chopped parsley

$^1/_3$ cup drained and chopped oil-packed sun-dried tomatoes

8 sheets phyllo pastry (thawed if frozen)

4 tablespoons ($^1/_2$ stick) butter, melted

Assorted crackers, for serving

1 pound green seedless grapes and dried mixed chopped fruits, for garnish

Grease a 15½ × 10½–inch jelly-roll pan. Preheat the oven to 375°F.

With a serrated knife, cut the wheel of Brie in half horizontally. Sprinkle the bottom half with the chopped parsley and dried tomatoes. Replace the top half.

Lay four sheets of phyllo dough on a work surface, overlapping to make one very large rectangle. Brush all four sheets with melted butter. Place the cheese in the center, and fold the sheets up, wrapping the Brie like a present. Set it aside; then lay out four more sheets, overlapping them as before. Brush the phyllo with butter. Invert the Brie, and set it in the center of the four sheets. Draw up the dough, gathering all the extra dough into the center, and scrunch it to form a flowerlike shape. The butter will help it all stick together.

Place the wrapped Brie in the center of a baking sheet. Bake until it is golden brown, about 25 minutes. Serve the baked Brie on a tray surrounded by crackers, grapes, and dried fruits.

the winner is

an oscar party

When one Ashland, Oregon, family's lifelong obsession with the movies turned professional, a fabulous neighborhood tradition was born. The family's son is now a well-known director. They held their first Oscar party when one of his films was up for an award. Potluck foods, voting in all categories, and goofy prizes donated and exchanged set the tone for the evening. The party is now fourteen years old and more fun than ever. The best "Oscar" prize is a six-foot metal suit of armor that the winner must take home and display on the lawn or porch until the following year. And that's the booby prize—for the person who misses the most in Ashland's own "Academy." Serious hissing and booing as well as tears and laughter ensue around the four or five televisions scattered in Jack and Claire's house. Some guests dress up in Oscar finery. Others come in black T-shirts. And everyone who wins thanks their mothers.

STRAWBERRY SHORTCAKE

makes 16 to 20 servings

It's so rare to see the real McCoy, your neighbors are bound to flip for these. Make smaller biscuits, and you can get more small servings. Make them the day you plan to serve and no earlier and serve warm if possible.

4 pints strawberries, rinsed, hulled, and quartered

$1/2$ cup plus 4 teaspoons sugar

2 cups heavy cream

$1/2$ teaspoon vanilla extract

24 Basic Sweet Biscuits (see opposite page), preferably hot out of the oven

6 tablespoons ($3/4$ stick) unsalted butter, melted

Toss the strawberries in a bowl with ½ cup of the sugar. Let them stand at room temperature for 2 hours, stirring occasionally.

Combine the cream with the vanilla and the remaining 4 teaspoons of sugar, and whip until it is thick but still soft. Cover the bowl loosely, and refrigerate it.

Just before serving, pull the hot biscuits in half, and brush the bottom halves with melted butter. Spoon some strawberries with their juice and a dollop (or two) of whipped cream onto each biscuit. Replace the biscuit tops at an angle and serve immediately.

Strawberry Porch Party

In upstate New York, twelve families wait in eager anticipation each spring for the call announcing the strawberries are ready to be picked. When the berries reach the moment of perfection, their determined women head out to pick dozens upon dozens of pints. They spend the next day canning and freezing the strawberries, but a few of the choicest are set aside for the Porch Party, at which fresh strawberry shortcake is served up for the whole neighborhood.

162 block parties & poker nights

basic sweet
biscuits

BASIC SWEET BISCUITS

makes 24 (1 1/2-inch) biscuits

Take care not to overwork the dough, and these will melt in your mouth.

- 1 3/4 cups all-purpose flour
- 2 tablespoons sugar
- 1 teaspoon salt
- 1 tablespoon double-acting baking powder
- 6 tablespoons (3/4 stick) unsalted butter, cut in chunks
- 3/4 cup cream

Preheat the oven to 450°F.

Combine the flour, sugar, salt, and baking powder in the food processor. Pulse to aerate the mixture.

Drop the butter into the flour mixture and process until it resembles coarse crumbs. Add the cream, and process just until the mixture forms a ball.

Turn the dough out onto a lightly floured board. Knead it quickly; then roll it out into a 6 × 8–inch rectangle. Cut the dough with a lightly floured biscuit cutter. Transfer the biscuits to a baking sheet, and don't allow the sides to touch.

Bake until the biscuits are lightly browned, 12 to 15 minutes.

summer

summer ◆ Many neighborhoods hold their block parties in early summer, but summer is also a time when families and friends gather to celebrate the Fourth of July, Labor Day, and just plain gorgeous weather. From parades to talent shows, from big grilling events to intimate beach parties, summer can be warm fun for all ages. Potluck makes summer parties manageable. The following tried-and-true summer recipes travel well.

FROZEN DAIQUIRIS

makes 12 servings

This makes a wonderful "slushy" daiquiri, all ready to serve. Using the limeade can to measure ingredients makes this concoction ridiculously simple to stir up.

1 (12-ounce) can frozen limeade concentrate
2 cans (3 cups) rum
3 cans (4½ cups) water

Pour all the ingredients into a container. Mix well and pour the drink into ice cube trays. Freeze it for at least 4 hours; it will freeze into a kind of slush.

When ready to serve the daiquiris, put the semifrozen mixture into a blender, and blend it briefly.

FROZEN LEMON MARGARITAS

margaritas margaritas makes 6 to 8 servings

If you can buy Meyer lemons from California, you'll discover the margarita has ascended to a whole new level!

2 lemon slices

Coarse salt

2 cups cracked ice

1¼ cups tequila

½ cup fresh lemon juice and grated zest of 1 lemon

⅓ cup orange liqueur

Strips of lemon zest, for garnish

Rub the rim of cocktail glasses with the lemon slices, and dip the glasses in salt.

Place the ice, tequila, lemon juice and zest, and liqueur in a blender. Cover, and blend until well mixed. Pour the margaritas into glasses, and garnish them with lemon zest strips.

PERFECT AND POTENT MARGARITAS

Refined after years of practice, this is my husband Todd's killer margarita recipe. Make a single drink or a big batch, just stick with this ratio of ingredients.

1 part white tequila

1 part gold tequila

1 part Rose's lime juice

1 part triple sec

2 parts Jose Cuervo margarita mix (or equivalent)

A splash of blue curaçao (to give the "pool water" green look)

Lime wedges

Salt (preferably margarita salt)

Crushed ice

Combine the tequilas, lime juice, triple sec, margarita mix, and curaçao in a pitcher. Wipe the rim of each serving glass with a wedge of lime. Invert the glass into a saucer of salt to coat the rim. Add crushed ice and pour the margarita.

FROZEN CHERRY MARGARITAS

frozen cherry margaritas

makes 6 servings

An unusual variation on the standard blend, these pretty pink cocktails get great flavor and texture from frozen fresh cherries.

1 cup fresh sweet Bing or Queen Anne cherries, pitted

6 ounces tequila

4 ounces triple sec or other orange liqueur

¼ cup fresh lime juice

2 tablespoons superfine sugar

2 teaspoons grenadine

4 cups ice

Cherries or lime slices, for garnish

Place the cherries in a single layer on a baking sheet. Place them in the freezer until frozen, about 2 hours.

Combine the frozen cherries, tequila, triple sec, lime juice, sugar, and grenadine in a blender. Blend for 2 minutes or until the mixture is smooth.

With the machine running, drop in ice through the small opening, stopping and scraping down the sides as needed.

(For margaritas with salt, dip the rims of chilled goblets in lime juice and then in coarse salt to coat the rims.) Pour the margaritas and garnish with fresh cherries or lime slices. Serve the drinks immediately.

SANGRIA FOR A CROWD

sangria

makes 100 (4-ounce) servings

This yields a great big batch, but it goes quickly. Buy a brand-new plastic garbage can for the sangria every summer.

1½ gallons dry red wine

1½ gallons fresh orange juice

1 cup sugar, or to taste

2 oranges, thinly sliced

2 lemons, thinly sliced

Enough ice to chill

Mix the wine, juice, and sugar. Stir well, and add more sugar if desired. Add the sliced fruit and ice. Serve the sangria cold.

memorial day

Every Monday on Memorial Day weekend, forty families who live in a neighborhood on the Long Island Sound venture down to the beach to welcome summer. It's a casual affair to which each family brings its own meal. But one year, Marybeth Connor added a twist. She went to the local bakery and ordered twenty sheet cakes with no icing, just yellow cake. She picked twenty families she knew would have fun with her unexpected task. She dropped the sheet cakes off with instructions. "Please decorate this cake by illustrating what summer means to your family." All twenty cakes were displayed on picnic tables down at the beach. From fancy drawings done in sugar icing to candy and toy decorations, each cake told a unique story. To add to the fun, families had to guess which cake was decorated by which family.

ROSY SANGRIA

rosy sangria

Here's a more elaborate sangria, appropriate for a smaller group. Use the ripest fruits you can find—peaches, nectarines, plums, or apricots. Your sangria will say "summer" all by itself.

1 cup water

½ cup sugar

3 lemon slices

3 whole cloves

1 cinnamon stick

4 blackberry herbal tea bags

1 (750-ml) bottle white zinfandel wine

2 tablespoons brandy

1 pint strawberries, hulled and sliced

¼ pound fresh sweet Bing or Queen Anne cherries, pitted

2 peaches, cut into 1-inch chunks

1 cup club soda or seltzer

Combine the water, sugar, lemon, cloves, and cinnamon stick in a small saucepan. Bring just to a simmer, and simmer for 10 minutes. Remove the pan from the heat. Add the tea bags and allow them to steep for 5 minutes. Remove and discard all solids; then refrigerate the tea mixture until it's cold.

In a large pitcher, stir together the tea mixture, wine, and brandy. Add the strawberries and cherries. Refrigerate, covered, from 4 to 48 hours.

Just before serving, stir in the peaches and club soda. Serve the sangria in chilled glasses, spooning some of the fruit in with the wine.

WATERMELON SLUSH

watermelon slush

makes 8 to 10 servings

A fresh, light drink, Watermelon Slush is perfect for summer festivities. For a large batch, watermelon cubes can be frozen in plastic freezer bags up to 2 months ahead. Chill champagne flutes in the freezer if you want a snazzier presentation.

4 cups watermelon cubes, seeded (about 8 ounces)

2 cups champagne

2 tablespoons fresh lemon juice

3 teaspoons superfine sugar, or to taste

Watermelon wedges and fresh mint leaves, for garnish

Place the watermelon cubes on a waxed-paper-lined baking sheet, and freeze the cubes until they're firm, about 20 minutes.

Combine the champagne, lemon juice, sugar, and 1 cup of frozen watermelon cubes in blender. Whirl until the mixture's smooth.

With the machine running, drop the remaining watermelon cubes through the opening. Whirl until the slush is smooth, scraping as needed.

Pour the drink immediately into chilled glasses. Garnish them with watermelon wedges and mint, and serve them with short straws.

MANGO CHICKEN SALAD

mango chicken salad

makes 6 to 8 servings

Pasta salads can be dull, but a sprightly citrus dressing and exotic mango make this one far from average.

2 cups cooked chicken breast meat, cubed

1 cup cooked rotini (corkscrew-shape pasta)

2 large ripe mangoes, peeled and cubed

1 teaspoon grated lemon zest

$1/4$ cup fresh orange juice

3 tablespoons fresh lime juice

3 tablespoons cooking oil

$1/4$ cup chopped fresh cilantro

$1/2$ large red onion, chopped

$1/2$ cup grated carrots

$1/2$ fresh jalapeño pepper, chopped, optional

Lettuce, for serving

Mix together the chicken, pasta, and mangoes in a large bowl. Add the lemon zest, fresh orange juice, lime juice, and oil, and toss to coat.

Add the cilantro, onion, carrots, and jalapeño, and toss again until well blended. Cover and refrigerate the mixture for 30 minutes to allow the flavors to blend. Serve this salad on individual beds of lettuce.

fourth of july
the mother lode

Some communities use Independence Day as the focus of a daylong activity-packed event. One I learned of in Maine involves over sixty families, a parade, a talent show, games, and a huge cookout, and has been held for almost forty years. While the day takes some organizing and planning, it's nothing that can't be handled just the week before. Year to year, minor changes take place, but as Jackie Morton, a participant of twenty-five years told me, "This would happen if no one lifted a finger—it's in the base of the pine trees."

Here's what the day looks like:

- 9 A.M.—The neighborhood parade starts. Kids, adults, and dogs alike march through the neighborhood and down to the common grass area for the flag-raising ceremony. Everyone recites the Pledge of Allegiance, and if there is willing local talent, songs are sung to the accompaniment of flutes, recorders, or trumpets. At this time, the roster for the first round of play in a tennis tournament is posted.

- 10 A.M.—The games begin, and the bake sale and raffle get under way. (Money from the bake sale and raffle go to help maintain a tennis court nearby.) The games include the Three-Legged Race, Sack Race, Egg Toss, and Water Balloon Toss, for eight and unders, nine- to thirteen-year-olds, and fourteen years and up. The final game is Tug-of-War—men against women. There was a time when this battle was contested over a pit dug that morning and filled with water, so losers were dragged through the mud. Today the event is a little cleaner.

- The games conclude with an award ceremony conducted on the spot with three-tiered cardboard boxes standing in for the awards podium, and medals for first, second, and third places. One year the medals were made of felt left over from the talent show. One year they were paper medals with the new Sacagawea dollar coin in the center.

- 11 A.M.—The Watermelon Hunt: All the kids gather around to listen to the reading of the first clue in this neighborhood-wide treasure hunt. Big kids help the little ones keep up as they run around the neighborhood looking for the slip of paper with the next clue. Five clues later, they arrive in someone's yard, usually a newcomer's, in search of the two hidden watermelons. Once found, they are immediately carved up and served!

- Noon — After the Watermelon Hunt, everyone takes a break. In the old days, it was a projector and film. Today, a couple of movies are rented, and young kids chill out for an hour as the older kids and adults continue a tennis tournament down by the commons.

- 1 P.M. — Tennis Tournament Finals get under way, with many neighbors congregating to cheer the finalists on.

- 3 P.M. — The Talent Show. This event has taken place in the same barn since the beginning. The big doors are swung open, and the sloping ramp becomes the stage area. The audience takes their seats in the driveway and are treated to short skits and plays, musical performances, baton-twirling, lip-syncing, and dance routines. The talent show concludes the very same way each year. Flowers are presented to the homeowner, now in her nineties; then one dad stands and raises his arm for attention. In unison, the entire audience recites, "This is the best talent show ever."

- 5 P.M. — The picnic gets going. Each family brings either a picnic table or card table and sets them up for a meal. A charcoal fire is lit in the communal grill that has been rented, while everyone sets out their own food. It's understood that everyone will try everyone else's appetizers, drinks, and snacks. A volleyball net is set up, and sometimes the nearby tennis court continues to see action, but for the most part, the picnic is a chance to review the day, catch up, and gab. This is also when the raffle drawing takes place. The items have ranged over the years from a bottle of wine or scented candles to services like lawn-mowing or baby-sitting, all donated by residents.

- 7 P.M. — The Flag Lowering. As the flag is lowered, often a kid with a trumpet or clarinet will have planted himself in the nearby woods to play taps. Sometimes a few more songs are sung. Finally, for as long as anyone can remember, there has been a special reading of a short essay written years ago by an English professor who lived in the neighborhood. The piece asks that we not forget why we gather to celebrate on the Fourth of July. It tells the story of how the Declaration of Independence came to be and what made this document so remarkable back then and why it remains so important today.

- A campfire is lit, and folks hang out for a few more hours, enjoying one another's company. By 9 P.M., the common ground is clear.

taco parfait
TACO PARFAIT

taco parfait

serves 24 guests

A heartier version of the perennially popular taco salad, this was one innovative cook's impressive presentation for her block party.

$^1/_2$ cup chopped onion

1 tablespoon vegetable oil

1 pound ground beef

$1^1/_2$ teaspoons salt

2 garlic cloves, minced (1 teaspoon)

1 (4-ounce) can diced green chiles

2 cups sour cream

1 package taco seasoning mix

$^1/_8$ teaspoon hot pepper sauce

1 (16-ounce) can Mexican-style refried beans

$^3/_4$ cup prepared guacamole, or 2 ripe avocados, mashed

1 cup shredded Cheddar or Monterey Jack cheese

2 medium tomatoes, chopped

$^1/_2$ cup sliced scallions

$^1/_2$ cup sliced black olives

Tortilla chips

In a skillet, cook the onion in the oil over medium-high heat until it is softened but not browned, about 5 minutes. Add the beef, salt, and garlic. Cook, stirring to break up the meat, until it is nicely browned and cooked through. Using a slotted spoon, transfer the mixture to a large bowl, and stir in the chiles.

In a small bowl, combine the sour cream and taco seasoning. Stir until they're blended. In another bowl, mix the hot sauce into the refried beans.

Spread the beans over the bottom of an 8-inch springform pan or a plate. Top with the meat mixture, then the seasoned sour cream, and the guacamole. Cover the pan with plastic wrap, pressing it onto the surface of the guacamole. Refrigerate until chilled, from 2 hours to 2 days.

Just before serving time, remove the plastic wrap, and carefully release the sides of the springform pan. Top with the cheese, tomatoes, scallions, and olives. Serve with a small knife to spread the parfait on the tortilla chips.

Potluck Pointers

- Remind people to put their names on the platters or bowls in which they brought food; that way, if they forget to retrieve them, the serving items can be returned at a later date.
- Food may sit out for a while, so avoid anything that might spoil. Salads with mayonnaise-based dressing should be refrigerated until you're ready to serve them; dump leftovers after an hour or so if the day is very hot and the food is unshaded.
- Serve finger and fork food only (no knives).
- Paper plates may be provided, but do tell people to bring their serving utensils. Label these, too, if they are not disposable.

BEER CAN CHICKEN

This recipe may sound silly, but the results are so delicious, you must give it a try. I always cook two chickens at once; the skins get good and crispy, and the evaporating beer keeps the birds moist. This is guaranteed fun for any gathering.

2 (12-ounce) cans beer

2 (3½- to 4-pound) chickens

½ cup of All-South Barbecue Rub (see opposite page), or a rub of your choice

Pop the tabs of each beer can. Pour off half the beer from each can, and discard (or drink) it. Set up the grill for indirect grilling with all the coals on one side of the grill and a drip pan on the other side. If you have a gas grill, set it on low.

Rinse the chickens and pat them dry with paper towels. Pull off and discard any fat. Sprinkle 1 teaspoon of the dry barbecue rub in the neck cavity and 2 teaspoons in the main cavity of each chicken. Add 1 tablespoon of the rub to each open can of beer. (Don't worry if it foams up.) Season the outside of each bird with 2 tablespoons of the rub.

Stand the beer cans on the work surface. Lower a chicken onto each can so that the can goes into the main cavity. Pull the chicken legs forward to form a sort of tripod: the chicken should sit upright over the can.

Carefully set the chickens on the grill in this position, placing them over the drip pan, away from the coals.

Barbecue the chickens until they're nicely browned and cooked through, about 1½ hours, keeping the temperature at about 350°F. (If you're using charcoal, replenish the coals as needed.) The internal temperature of the birds (taken in the thickest part of the thigh) should be at least 165°F.

Carefully transfer the birds to a platter in the same position, and let them stand for 10 minutes or so. Lift the bird off the can, discard the can, and carve as usual.

ALL-SOUTH BARBECUE RUB

makes about 1 cup

This makes plenty for 2 chickens. It is also great on pork or beef.

2 tablespoons salt

2 tablespoons granulated sugar

2 tablespoons brown sugar

2 tablespoons ground cumin

2 tablespoons chili powder

2 tablespoons cracked black pepper

1 tablespoon cayenne pepper

¼ cup paprika

Throw all the ingredients together in a bowl, and mix them well. Store the barbecue rub in a covered jar.

PEGGY MILLS' OCEAN REEF CHICKEN

Nestle this dish in a basket filled with crumpled newspaper for insulation, and your summer dinner is set to travel.

3 (2½-pound) chickens, cut into serving pieces

2 cups buttermilk

½ pound (2 sticks) butter

½ teaspoon dried tarragon

3 tablespoons fresh lemon juice

4 cups fine bread crumbs

¼ cup minced fresh parsley

½ cup sesame seeds

3 tablespoons seasoned salt

Rinse the chicken pieces, and then pat dry. Place the chicken in a shallow dish, pour buttermilk over it, cover tightly with plastic wrap, and refrigerate it overnight.

The next day, pour off and discard the buttermilk. Pat the chickens with dry paper towels.

Melt the butter in a saucepan; stir in the tarragon and lemon juice. In a shallow bowl combine the bread crumbs, parsley, sesame seeds, and seasoned salt; mix well.

Dip the chicken pieces in the melted butter; then roll it in the crumb mixture to coat thoroughly.

Arrange the chicken in a large baking dish in a single layer. Drizzle the remaining butter evenly over all the pieces. Cover the chicken tightly and refrigerate it until 1½ hours before serving time.

Preheat the oven to 350°F.

Bake the chicken in the oven without turning until it is golden and fork-tender, about 1½ hours. Serve this dish hot, warm, or at room temperature.

Under the Stars

Allan Jay makes campsite reservations every spring for twenty-five sites at a state park near his home in New England. It's always for the same date, and all the dads in his neighborhood bring their kids. Any child six years or older is welcome. The group heads out on Friday afternoon and returns late on Sunday; in between there is swimming, campfire cooking, nature walks, ghost stories, and the kind of long conversations between neighbors that you can't have at a cocktail party.

i love a parade

I have been to half a dozen Fourth of July parades, and the ones I love best are the neighborhood ones. Everyone who can walk or be pushed takes part, and the parade itself is appealingly homespun—and usually quite brief. Some conclude with a lunchtime barbecue.

If you want to start a parade in your neighborhood, send out a flyer with starting point and time and a route, and let the fun go from there. On the flyer include suggestions:

- Ask kids to decorate their bikes, wagons, and carts.
- Encourage everyone to dress up.
- Decorate the pet (who should be on a leash).
- Solicit ideas. Does anyone play a marching band instrument? Are there jugglers, gymnasts, or unicyclists on the block? Make all creative efforts welcome.

Get things going by buying and sharing with the neighbors:

- Enough small flags to go around
- Red, white, and blue streamers
- Cheap, plastic kazoos
- Small wrapped candies to be tossed to onlookers
- Helium balloons
- Small prizes for all entrants

The first year may be small, but you'll have set the stage for a fun and funny annual observance. Most parades I've attended are such small-scale events they don't bother getting a permit, but if yours is a busy area, plan ahead with your local authorities. Obviously it's best to avoid busy streets and stick to the sidewalks if traffic is an issue.

In Southern California, one cul-de-sac community boasts a view of several area fireworks displays, which punctuates their yearly celebration of the Fourth.

A few minutes before 9 P.M., each person carries a lawn chair (and someone brings a boom box) to the end of the block. Once settled, they watch the simultaneous fireworks displays synchronized to music on a local radio station. The view is wonderful, there are no crowds to battle, and when it's all over, everyone can walk home. After the kids are in bed, the adults bring out a portable fire pit, someone makes coffee, and they all stay out talking until very late.

WILD RICE AND CRAB CASSEROLE

casserole

makes 8 to 10 servings

My sister-in-law Kim Caldwell brought this once to the Fourth of July picnic in her community, and now it is a must each summer. It's got a few twists on the original, which was handed down from *Tidewater on the Half Shell*, the popular cookbook by the Junior League of Norfolk and Virginia Beach, Virginia.

1 cup wild rice

1 cup mayonnaise

1½ cups milk or cream

2 tablespoons Durkee Hot Sauce or 1 tablespoon Dijon mustard combined with 1 tablespoon mayonnaise

1 tablespoon Worcestershire sauce

½ teaspoon Tabasco sauce

1 tablespoon fresh lemon juice

1 tablespoon finely grated onion

1 pound fresh crabmeat, picked over

4 ounces sharp Cheddar cheese, grated

1 tablespoon chopped fresh parsley

Combine the 1 cup of rice with 4 cups of barely salted water in a saucepan. Bring the water to a boil, cover the pan, and simmer until tender, about 40 minutes. Drain the rice.

Preheat the oven to 350°F.

In a mixing bowl, whisk together the mayonnaise, milk, Durkee sauce, Worcestershire, Tabasco, lemon juice, and grated onion. Stir in the rice, crab, grated Cheddar, and chopped parsley.

Pour the mixture into a lightly greased casserole dish, and bake, uncovered, until it is golden brown, about 45 minutes. Serve warm.

WEEKLONG BEANS

weeklong
beans

makes 12 servings

This recipe is so named because you can make a big batch on a weekend and serve it a few more times over the course of a week. It's a salad in its own right, but leftovers are wonderful rolled up in a flour tortilla with some shredded cooked meat and your favorite cheese.

1 (30-ounce) can black beans, drained and rinsed

3½ cups diced fresh plum tomatoes or 1 (28-ounce) can diced tomatoes, drained

3 to 4 scallions, chopped, including 3 inches of green stem

1 large red bell pepper, cored, seeded, and diced

½ cup chopped fresh cilantro

½ cup extra virgin olive oil

Juice of 1 large lemon

Salt, pepper, and minced garlic to taste

In a large glass or ceramic bowl, combine the drained beans, tomatoes, scallions, diced red pepper, and cilantro. Mix lightly to combine the ingredients. Add the oil, lemon juice, and seasonings.

Mix again, and cover the beans for at least an hour before serving them. This is actually better if it is refrigerated as long as 24 hours before serving time.

VARIATION

Substitute one 15-ounce can black beans and one 15-ounce can white beans for the large can of black beans. Use yellow or orange peppers to vary the color; or use a combination of bell peppers, varying the amount to fit the recipe. Add pimientos or salad olives before serving, and mix well.

labor day

Like the Fourth of July, Labor Day sees many families traveling. However, in some communities school is well under way, so fewer people leave town. If your area is one of these, Labor Day might make a great time to start an annual neighborhood event. Many that I have come across involve daylong events such as talent shows and games. One of the oldest I came across is in Ohio, where Franny Taft has been running the show since it began in the fall of 1949. That year a small group of couples joined forces to establish a neighborhood that celebrated contemporary architecture as well as ethnic diversity. With sixty-five acres of farmland near Cleveland, they set about creating a community free of "imitation"-style homes. Now, over fifty years later, three generations of families that have been raised in Pepper Ridge spend leisure time together. One tradition stands above all others—the Labor Day weekend Pepper Ridge Summer Olympics.

Events include the expected tennis and swimming matches, but several rather unique "sports" have emerged over the years. An early addition was the building tournament, in which teams stack cardboard boxes as high as possible. An established artist and sculptor became the judge of the sculpting contest, in which entrants are given vegetables and a few paring knives from which to make their masterpiece. (To date, no one has surpassed the Loch Ness monster sculpture created in 1963 using a sliced summer squash and a pane of glass as a base. When the natural curve of a squash met the tinted glass, it matched perfectly that infamous photo!)

To celebrate the fiftieth anniversary of the Pepper Ridge Olympics, Franny, now eighty-five, organized a reunion. More than 125 adults and kids came for the weekend, and three generations celebrated with sack races, cookouts, and all the long-cherished traditions that Franny has nurtured.

SUSIE'S CHERRY CHICKEN SALAD

cherry chicken salad

makes 6 servings

My friend Susie Taylor lived in Traverse City, Michigan. Thanks to her, we always have a supply of that state's exceptional dried cherries, the secret ingredient in this recipe. If you can't find dried cherries, substitute dried cranberries or chopped Granny Smith apples.

1 store-bought rotisserie chicken, or 3 cups cooked, cubed chicken

1 cup mayonnaise

1 teaspoon fresh lemon juice

1 cup chopped celery

$^1/_4$ cup sliced almonds

$^3/_4$ cup dried cherries

Lettuce

Pull off and discard the skin from the chicken. Remove all the meat from the bones, and cut it into cubes. Place the chicken cubes in a large mixing bowl.

Add the remaining ingredients, and toss together until thoroughly mixed. Refrigerate this salad for at least 2 hours, and serve it chilled.

PITA AND CHEESE ROLL-UPS

makes 24 servings as an appetizer

Mild green sprouts in creamy white cheese rolled in a pita makes a yummy bite to pop in your mouth! For an authentic Middle Eastern touch, use yogurt cheese; it's available at Middle Eastern specialty grocers, but it's also quite easy to make yourself.

3 (6-inch) plain or whole-wheat pita breads

2 cups yogurt cheese (see below) or 16 ounces softened cream cheese combined with 1 tablespoon yogurt

¾ cup alfalfa sprouts

Split the pita bread to form 6 rounds. (If the bread is not pliable, soften it between damp towels for a few minutes.) Place the rounds with the inside up on a clean work surface. Spread each with about ⅓ cup yogurt cheese. Top each of the pitas with 2 tablespoons of the alfalfa sprouts.

Roll the pitas like jelly rolls, gently working out any air pockets. Wrap the roll-ups securely in plastic wrap, and refrigerate them for 1 hour, or overnight.

Remove the wrap, and trim the ends of the roll-ups with a serrated knife. Cut the rolls diagonally into ¾-inch slices. Arrange the pinwheels on a platter, and serve them chilled.

To Make Yogurt Cheese

Line a fine strainer with two layers of cheesecloth or a paper coffee filter. Empty a sixteen-ounce container of plain yogurt (low-fat, if you prefer) into the strainer, and place it over a bowl to catch the drips. Cover and refrigerate the yogurt for several hours (or overnight) to allow the liquid to drain. Use the yogurt cheese within two or three days.

TART AND CREAMY SPINACH-AND-HERB DIP

makes 4 cups

Surround a bowl of creamy dip with crunchy vegetables: carrot sticks, grape tomatoes, fennel, celery sticks, and yellow and zucchini squash fingers.

1 (10-ounce) package frozen chopped spinach, thawed and drained

1 cup mayonnaise

1 cup sour cream

$^1/_2$ cup chopped scallions

$^1/_4$ cup chopped parsley or cilantro

1 tablespoon fresh lemon or lime juice

1 tablespoon chopped fresh dill (1 teaspoon dried)

1 teaspoon salt

$^1/_2$ teaspoon freshly ground pepper

In a medium bowl, combine all the ingredients, and mix until they're well blended. Transfer the dip to a serving bowl, and cover it. Refrigerate it for at least 2 hours. This dip keeps well for up to 2 days.

SUMMER BERRY PIE

Jo McBrien, an old family friend, shared this recipe with us years ago. It's the best way to enjoy summer berries. You can certainly make your favorite pastry crust recipe if you are feeling ambitious, but a refrigerator crust will be just fine, too.

- 3/4 cup sugar
- 1/4 teaspoon salt
- 2 tablespoons cornstarch
- 2/3 cup boiling water
- 4 cups raspberries, blueberries, or blackberries—or any combination of the three
- 2 tablespoons butter
- 1 1/2 teaspoons fresh lemon juice
- 1 (9-inch) pie shell, baked and cooled
- Whipped cream, for serving

Stir together the sugar, salt, and cornstarch in a small saucepan. Add the boiling water, and cook over medium heat, stirring constantly until the mixture is thickened.

Add 1 cup of the berries, the butter, and the lemon juice. Stir the mixture, then cool it to lukewarm. In a mixing bowl, combine the sugar mixture with the remaining berries, and set it aside to cool completely.

Pour the filling into the baked pie shell. Chill until the filling is set, at least 1 hour. Add a dollop of whipped cream to each serving.

fall

fall ◆ For most folks, fall is a time of falling leaves. For my mother, it was a time to turn over a new leaf. With six kids, a dog, and other small pets, she was constantly trying to get or stay organized. By the end of the summer any semblance of routine had fallen by the wayside, so each September, my mother would outline How It Would Be. From room cleaning and laundry systems, to homework rules and piano practice, we were to Shape Up. I think neighborhoods go through some of this, too. The end of summer signals time for getting things done. With the worst of the heat behind us, outdoor chores can be tackled: storm windows are hung, flower beds cleared, leaves raked (and raked and raked). As in the spring, it makes sense to find ways to make big chores more manageable, and that's where the neighbors come in. All the families pitch in to clean up fallen branches, clean out gutters, mend fences or walls, and host yard sales. Halloween and Thanksgiving also offer great opportunities for friends and family to gather. For all the fall events, I've pulled together foolproof recipes for soup meals that warm body and soul.

BUTTERNUT SQUASH SOUP

My friend Stacey Anderson makes this with store-bought vinaigrette, and if you do the same, no one will be the wiser.

2 medium butternut squash

1 tablespoon olive oil

1/2 cup chopped onion

1 cup milk

1 teaspoon dried tarragon

1 cup Gingery Vinaigrette (see page 190)

1 cup chopped crystallized ginger, for garnish

1/4 cup chives, for garnish

Peel and cube the squash. Steam it over boiling water until tender, about 15 minutes. While the squash cooks, heat the oil in a skillet. Add the onions, and sauté them over medium-high heat for 5 minutes, or until they're softened.

Put the squash and some of the milk in a blender, and process until they're blended but not pureed. Add the rest of the milk, the onion, tarragon, and vinaigrette, and blend to a pleasing consistency.

Serve garnished with a sprinkling of crystallized ginger and chives.

GINGERY VINAIGRETTE

makes about 1 ³/₄ cups

1 (2-inch) piece ginger, peeled

¹/₄ teaspoon dried rosemary

2 garlic cloves

¹/₂ cup rice wine vinegar

¹/₄ cup soy sauce

2 tablespoons honey

1 cup peanut oil

A few drops of sesame oil

Chop the ginger, rosemary, and garlic in a food processor. Add the vinegar, soy sauce, and honey, and continue to blend. With the motor running, drizzle in the peanut and sesame oils until blended and emulsified.

cookie box day

Shore Acres in Mamaroneck, New York, is dense with families and kids. Lisa Nee wanted to make sure her oldest son felt as comfortable as possible on his first day of kindergarten. To help her son understand who was going to be in school with him and to help her get to know the moms, Lisa invited all fourteen kindergartners in the neighborhood and their mothers over to her house the day before school started, to make cookies and fancy cookie boxes for their classrooms. With two teenage girls hired to help, Lisa had one table set with the shoeboxes, white paper precut to cover the boxes, and lots of stickers, markers, glue sticks, and colored paper (no glitter—too messy!). In the kitchen, she had set out dough she had made over the weekend, along with cookie cutters shaped like schoolhouses, leaves, feet, and other silly shapes. Once everyone had decorated his or her cookie box and cut out cookies, she sent them outside for cider and some runaround time while the cookies baked—eighty in all. The kids returned to the house to decorate the baked cookies, each getting one-quarter cup of frosting to color as they chose (an adult should actually wield the food coloring).

Lisa knew which kids shared teachers, and she made sure that each classroom would receive enough boxes of cookies so that all the students could enjoy a cookie on their first day of school.

And Once School Has Started

One neighborhood holds an annual lunch for parents on the first day of school for all those who feel suddenly liberated.

SEAFOOD SOUP SUPREME

makes 24 servings

Bookbinders, a Philadelphia restaurant, started making this kind of rich, savory soup at least one hundred years ago, and it's still on the menu, still delicious! It's a great dish to serve at a large party. Get out your biggest soup pot and go.

- ¹/₄ pound (1 stick) butter
- ¹/₂ cup flour
- 1 pound chopped clams
- 3 cups fresh seafood pieces (such as snapper, whitefish, cod)
- 2 cups chopped celery
- 1 cup chopped carrots
- 1 cup chopped onion
- 1 tablespoon beef base
- 1 teaspoon salt
- 1 teaspoon marjoram
- 1 teaspoon seasoned salt
- 1 teaspoon Worcestershire sauce

  Salt and freshly ground black pepper to taste
- 1 (12-ounce) can tomato puree

  Good dry sherry, optional

Melt the butter in a heavy cast-iron or enamel skillet. Add the flour, and cook and stir over medium heat until the flour gives off a hearty aroma. Continue to cook until the roux is a deep mahogany color, watching carefully to ensure it does not burn. Set the roux aside.

Bring 4 quarts of water to a boil in a large pot. Add the clams and fish, and boil them for 15 minutes. Add the vegetables and all the seasonings. Reduce the heat, and simmer for 30 minutes.

Add the tomato puree, and cook for another 30 minutes. Ladle 1 cup of the hot liquid into the roux, and whisk until the mixture is smooth. Whisk the roux into the soup, a little at a time, and cook just until the soup has a creamy consistency. Adjust the seasonings to your taste.

Offer the sherry in cruets at each table as an optional addition to each bowl when serving.

giant garage sale

I know of several neighborhoods that organize garage sales in the fall every other year or so. It keeps the clutter down and is a great way to spend a Saturday morning. Depending on how many neighbors choose to participate, you'll need some good organization. Pick a Saturday after Labor Day, send around a sign-up sheet, and if you think there might be some special items, try to find out in time for them to be mentioned in the local paper. When the last pair of old golf clubs or battered two-wheeler finds a home, count your earnings over a lunch of chili and corn bread.

tortilla soup

CHERI ALLEN'S
TORTILLA SOUP

makes 20 servings

Cheri introduced us to many of our neighbors over steaming servings of this delicious meal-in-a-bowl. To cut the tortillas easily, just stack them, and slice them into French-fry-size pieces. Two roast chickens from the refrigerator case or rotisserie counter will yield enough cooked meat for this recipe. You can save more time by substituting crumbled tortilla chips for the fried tortilla strips.

- 1 large onion, diced
- 1 tablespoon minced garlic (6 cloves)
- 3 tablespoons vegetable oil
- 2 cups chopped green chiles from a jar or can
- 2 quarts chicken stock
- 5 tomatoes, diced
- 1 quart tomato juice
- 24 corn tortillas, cut into strips
- 5 to 6 cups coarsely chopped cooked chicken
   Juice of 6 limes
- 3 cups grated Monterey Jack or Cheddar cheese
   Zest of 2 limes

In a large pot, sauté the onion and garlic in 1 tablespoon of the oil until they're translucent, about 5 minutes. Add the chiles, and sauté for 3 more minutes. Add the chicken stock, tomatoes, and tomato juice, and bring to a boil. Simmer for 10 minutes.

While the soup simmers, heat the remaining 2 tablespoons of oil in a large skillet. Add the tortilla strips a handful at a time, tossing them over high heat until they're crisp. Drain the cooked strips on paper towels, and repeat with the remaining strips, adding more oil as needed.

Add the salt and cooked chicken to the soup, and then stir in the lime juice to taste.

Place some of the tortilla strips in the bottom of each bowl. Ladle the soup over them, and garnish with a sprinkle of cheese and the lime zest.

SPICED CRANBERRY CIDER
cider

makes 8 to 10 servings

Serve this warm to leaf rakers, apple pickers, or tailgaters when the weather turns nippy. It smells wonderful.

  2 quarts unfiltered apple cider
  1/4 cup cranberry juice cocktail concentrate, frozen or from a can
  1 cinnamon stick
  3 cloves
  3 cardamom pods, optional
  2 strips orange peel

Combine all the ingredients in a saucepan and heat just to a simmer over medium-high heat. Simmer for 5 or 10 minutes, until very fragrant. Serve hot in mugs.

halloween

Who doesn't love Halloween? Until recently trick-or-treating had declined some-what, thanks to alarming media reports of potential dangers to kids, but I see a big comeback of locally organized Halloween events, and I'm delighted. I grew up trick-or-treating, and it was the highlight of my year. Carving pumpkins, making costumes, and advising my mom on what candy to buy—it was all great stuff. Today kids start earlier in the night, and many towns have a curfew, but fortunately the fun is back.

Whether your kids are into it or not, let the neighborhood know if you're a Halloween lover. Decorate your house. In some neighborhoods not only is that a must, it's also an obsession. I'm personally not too keen on mannequins dangling by a rope from the window or severed heads swinging from trees, but I've seen plenty of both in otherwise quiet, staid neighborhoods. I love the clever decorations.

One friend turns her second-floor windows into yellow cat eyes, and at night it is really effective. If you don't want to be the only one on your block to suddenly get ghoulish, enlist a few people to get the ball rolling. In just a few years, the whole street can be terrifying.

At the very least, carve a pumpkin. There are plenty of patterns, but all that's really necessary is a good sharp knife, a scraping spoon, and some muscle. If you do plan to carve a few pumpkins, consider inviting neighbors over who don't have kids. It's one of the nicest things you can do. They'll enjoy having their own pumpkin to light on Halloween night.

Here are a few pumpkin tips:

- The lid should have a notch cut out that acts as a chimney.

- Votive candles work well. Consider nestling them in a loose wad of foil—it helps to stabilize them. Those disposable neon necklaces that kids love can also light up a pumpkin safely.

- Light them only on Halloween night, and carve them only days before—they rot quickly.

- Squirrels love pumpkins. Don't be surprised if they get to yours.

- Decaying pumpkins make great fertilizer. Break yours up, and spread them around in your garden to contribute nutrients for the winter.

Halloween Night

Trick-or-treating offers you a chance to say hello to neighbors you may not have met or barely know. It's not a time for long chats, but consider doing more than just giving out candy. Many young kids who trick-or-treat are accompanied by an adult or two. Walk outside so you can say hello to the adult who is waiting for a child to choose her treat. Introduce yourself. Ask where they live. Offer cider or a beer to the adult. In one neighborhood of brownstones, everyone sits right out on their steps next to their pumpkin and bowl of candy. There's plenty of chatter back and forth while waiting for the goblins and vampires to arrive.

If you live in a condominium or apartment building, consider posting a sign-up sheet so people know what doors are okay to knock on as well as which kids will be trick-or-treating.

There are lots of ways to make the night more fun:

- If you're the one dispensing candy, wear a costume.
- Exchange the regular door or porch light for an orange or purple bulb.
- Play scary music or creepy sound effects.
- Serve the candy from a bowl or cauldron you've decorated.
- Set dry ice in a bucket near the front door for the haunted house effect.
- Put a costume on your dog.

Whether homemade or store-bought (check catalogs, too), these decorations will get you in the Halloween spirit:

- The witch who's crashed into the tree
- Dancing ghosts made of sheets
- Tombstones with funny inscriptions
- Wicked-witch feet coming out from under the porch wall
- Black cats dancing across the yard
- Newspaper-stuffed figures made of old clothes, topped with a pumpkin head
- Bats trapped in spiderwebs that cover the front door

A clever friend of mine decorates her pumpkins entirely with vegetables. Halved bell peppers become ears, kale serves as hair, and cauliflower, broccoli, beans, and raisins are just some of the foods that make the features. Toothpicks help keep it all together.

SPIDER SANDWICHES

makes 8 servings

If you have Halloween cookie cutters, use them to cut out other fun and spooky shapes like bats or black cats for pre-trick-or-treating snacks.

16 slices whole-wheat bread or pumpernickel cocktail breads

1 cup peanut butter

1 1/2 cups chocolate-hazelnut spread or grape jelly

Black licorice laces

Red hot candies

Spread half the bread slices with the peanut butter, then spread the remainder with the chocolate-hazelnut spread or jelly. Assemble the sandwiches, then use a large round cutter (or other shapes) to cut out circles. Insert eight 2-inch lengths of licorice lace, four on each side, between the bread layers to form spider legs. Use a dab of peanut butter to stick on two red hots for eyes.

it's a scary parade!

In Indian Village, a notice goes out about a week before Halloween reminding families with small kids that the annual Halloween parade begins at 3:30 P.M. Each year about forty-five very young children dressed as peanuts, pumpkins, Draculas, princesses, and bugs, and their parents, gather for a very brief but hugely popular parade. Those goblins who can't walk arrive in strollers, wagons, and pushcarts.

The event starts with a group photo, and then the parade begins. For three blocks this colorful collection of kids walks to the big bend in the street, where tables filled with sandwiches and juice await. Parents get a chance to see all the cute costumes before it's too dark, and the kids get some nutritious food in their tummies before the candy frenzy begins.

HALLOWEEN SWEET POTATO SALAD

makes 8 to 10 servings

The orange and black colors of this salad make it perfect for Halloween, but its sweet, spicy flavor is also delicious in the summertime.

1 cup raisins

2 pounds sweet potatoes, peeled and cut into 1-inch chunks

5 carrots, grated

$1/3$ cup extra virgin olive oil

3 tablespoons fresh lime juice

1 teaspoon chili powder

$1/2$ teaspoon ground cumin

Salt and pepper to taste

Soak the raisins in hot water to cover for 30 minutes to soften. Drain.

Cook the sweet potatoes in a large saucepan of boiling water over high heat for 7 to 10 minutes, or until tender but not mushy. Drain thoroughly and place in a large bowl with the carrots and drained raisins.

Whisk the olive oil, lime juice, chili powder, cumin, and salt and pepper together in a small bowl. Pour over the salad and toss gently to combine. Season with salt and pepper to taste.

RICHARD'S VEGETABLE CHILI

makes 8 servings

My brother-in-law is famous for his chili, which has even meat-eaters lining up for seconds. The bulgur gives the dish enough heft that you don't miss the meat. If you want to serve a bigger crowd, just double all the ingredients.

- ³/₄ cup bulgur
- 2 tablespoons vegetable oil
- 2 large onions, chopped
- 2 garlic cloves, minced (1 teaspoon)
- 1 cup chopped celery
- 1 cup chopped carrots
- 1 cup chopped green bell pepper
- 1 (28-ounce) can tomatoes with juices (whole or crushed but without added puree)
- 2 (14-ounce) cans kidney beans, drained
- 2 tablespoons chili powder
- 1 to 2 tablespoons fresh lemon juice
- 1 teaspoon ground cumin
- ¼ teaspoon crushed red pepper flakes
- 1 whole jalapeño pepper, seeded and finely diced (for a smokier flavor, you may substitute 1 chipotle, also seeded and diced)

In a saucepan, combine the bulgur and 2 cups of water. Bring it to a boil; then turn off the heat, and let it stand for 6 minutes. Drain off any excess water.

Heat the oil in a large pot. Add the onions, garlic, celery, carrots, and green pepper, and sauté the mixture over medium heat until the onions are tender, about 5 minutes. Add the tomatoes, kidney beans, chili powder, lemon juice, cumin, red pepper flakes, and jalapeño pepper. Cover and simmer the chili for 10 minutes, or until the vegetables are tender. Add the cooked bulgur. If the mixture is too thick, add a bit of water. Simmer for another 5 minutes. Adjust the seasoning by adding hot sauce or more pepper flakes, or salt and pepper.

Serve the chili immediately. Leftovers freeze well.

Thanksgiving

If you are hosting Thanksgiving for your family or extended family, take a moment to consider if there is someone in your neighborhood who has no Thanksgiving plans. They might love an invitation to join yours. It's the perfect time to include all the strays, singles, and students who can't go home for the holidays. Although Thanksgiving often focuses on family gatherings, many neighborhoods have a traditional Turkey Bowl football game the next day. If you have been looking for a way to get the guys to gather, this may be just the thing to try.

HOT AND SASSY CORN BREAD

makes 8 portions

Add this to your chili night, or to any soup dish.

1 1/2 cups yellow cornmeal

1/2 cup unbleached flour

1 teaspoon baking powder

3/4 teaspoon salt

1/2 teaspoon baking soda

1 tablespoon brown sugar

1 tablespoon granulated sugar

1 cup canned creamed corn

1/2 cup sour cream

1/2 cup milk

2 eggs, lightly beaten

2 tablespoons vegetable oil

4 fresh jalapeño peppers, seeded and chopped

Preheat the oven to 400°F. Butter an 8-inch square baking pan.

In a medium bowl, mix together the cornmeal, flour, baking powder, salt, baking soda, and sugars.

In another bowl, stir the corn, sour cream, milk, eggs, oil, and jalapeños. Mix until smooth.

Add half the liquid mixture to the dry mixture and stir until it is just blended. Add the remaining liquid, and stir just until blended. Pour the batter into the prepared pan.

Bake the bread until the top is golden and a knife inserted in the center comes out clean, about 25 minutes. Cool it slightly in the pan before cutting it into squares.

blooming success
a plant exchange

If your neighborhood is fairly well established, chances are many homeowners have mature garden plantings that could benefit from division. Why not hold a plant-sharing event at which neighbors can swap plants they don't need or want for those they do? It's a wonderful way to expand your own garden with new plants at no cost and just as good a reason to pare down overgrown perennials. Many early-blooming plants can be divided in fall, but some should be transplanted in spring. Check a gardening resource if you're not sure.

Here's how to get started:

- Every neighborhood seems to come with one individual who has a truly green thumb. Ask him or her to help organize the event and identify overgrown plantings.

- Determine the best weekend; then set a time for the actual digging and exchanging. Allow at least two full hours.

- In advance buy peat moss, fertilizer, and dry manure, and split the cost among the participants. Put them in a wheelbarrow, cart, or kid's wagon for transport.

- Determine which plants people want to share. This can be established by a casual call or a sign-up sheet. Make sure new neighbors (who may have less-established gardens) know about the event.

- As a group, do all the digging first; migrate from garden bed to garden bed. Use wet newspaper to wrap and cover roots.

- Assemble what has been dug up in a central location. (If you cannot immediately plant what has been dug up, you'll need to pot them.)

- Divide up the plantings. As a group, replant the plants in the selected gardens, enriching the soil with fertilizer, manure, or peat moss as needed.

- Once you're all working together, you may also want to help one another plant some bulbs. It's also a good time to exchange cuttings of tender annuals to cultivate indoors over the winter for spring replanting. Coleus, geranium, and wax begonia are good candidates.

MOM'S APPLE PIE

apple pie

If your mother or grandmother was renowned for her apple pie, then this straightforward but infallible version will taste like home to you. A scoop of good-quality vanilla ice cream makes it company food.

crust

2¼ cups all-purpose flour, unsifted

½ pound (2 sticks) cold, unsalted butter

¼ cup vegetable shortening

½ teaspoon salt

5 to 6 tablespoons ice water

filling

6 to 9 firm, tart apples, such as Granny Smith or Cortland

2 tablespoons flour

Cinnamon to taste

½ cup granulated sugar

½ cup packed brown sugar

To prepare the crust, place the flour, butter, shortening, and salt in a food processor, and process just until it is crumbly. With the processor running, add the ice water, 1 tablespoon at a time, just until the dough forms a loose ball.

Remove the dough, form it into a ball, cover it with waxed paper or plastic wrap, and chill it for at least 20 minutes before rolling.

Meanwhile, make the filling: Slice the apples thinly. Toss them with the flour, cinnamon, and sugars.

Divide the dough into 2 pieces, and roll the top and bottom crusts. Line the bottom crust on a 9-inch pie pan, and fill it with the apple filling. Top with the second crust. Flute the edges, and cut 2 or 3 vents in the top crust.

Preheat the oven to 450°F.

Bake the pie for 10 minutes; then reduce the heat to 350°F, and continue baking until the crust is golden, about 30 more minutes. Cool the pie on a rack. Cut it into wedges, and serve it with vanilla ice cream or a slice of Cheddar cheese.

traditions
letting go and reinventing

I heard of one neighborhood in which a long-standing annual event sputtered out and died after the woman who organized it moved from the neighborhood and turned it over to a group of women. People were disappointed and suggested that the original hostess had wasted her time establishing the event because it hadn't lasted. I disagree. Fifteen years is a good run. Often some of the most inventive parties are spearheaded by a single individual who has a gift for throwing clever parties. That kind of party is really hard to pass along, especially to a committee. Traditions can be sustained only by people who care, and those who care enough to continue a tradition should have the right and the room to transform and update it. Besides, annual is a relative term. Sometimes good parties need a rest. Reviving themes and events years later can be as much fun as inventing them from scratch.

Winter

winter ◆ In wintertime, cooler temperatures and holiday obligations tend to keep us behind closed doors. There are fewer chance encounters on the soccer fields or over leaf raking, and even the dog walkers tend to keep their strolls short and to the point—no lingering on street corners. With so many pressing family matters, it's easy to put neighborhood activities on the back burner until the warm weather lures us all outdoors again in the spring.

Make the extra effort to bring folks together and to incorporate your neighbors into your holiday rituals. It makes the holidays that much more meaningful, and further strengthens the bonds between community members when they share these wonderful times together. Don't forget those who might not have family nearby; now, more than ever, they need to feel included and cared for.

Aside from the progressive dinners that often take place in January or February, holiday entertaining dominates much of this season. There are creative and easy ways to make this time of year special for a neighborhood, on a big scale or a small one.

I have lived in neighborhoods that consider white candle lights in each window the standard for Christmas decorating. I have also lived in neighborhoods where five strands of Christmas lights is the sign of a lazy homeowner. It's hard to buck the trend when it comes to those outdoor lights. How crazy you want to go depends on how much you want to fit in—or stand out.

There is, however, an outdoor lighting event that is as special as any I have seen. It is magical, beautiful, silent, and rare. On Christmas Eve, brown paper lunch bags and a bucket of sand are dropped off at every single house on Ashland Street in Wilmette, Illinois, between the railroad tracks and Lake Michigan. This street runs straight for more than one mile, with homes tightly packed on both sides. At dusk, each homeowner sets out a line of paper bags, each weighted with sand and holding a votive candle. The candles are lit and left to burn through the night. Over the years, parallel streets and side streets have joined in the tradition. To walk or drive through these streets on Christmas Eve is to be reminded that a simple effort shared by many can be worth so much more than any individual's. I challenge any adult to experience this lovely display with a dry eye.

It's true that the holiday season, despite the commercialism and pressure to get it all done, is one that brings out the very best in all of us. We seem more willing to greet and give to others. So try to carve out some time for homemade holiday gifts, and plan an event to make the most of the season. Some I like are the cookie exchange, a caroling party, and a New Year's Day open house. Whichever you choose, use this time of the year to reestablish bonds and make new ones.

sweet times

a cookie exchange

When you go to Christy Hipp's Cookie Exchange Party, not only do you have to bring a few dozen cookies, you also have to bring your own plastic storage containers. About twenty-five women gather on a December evening for coffee, talk, and cookies. During the party, each person walks through the dining room, where all the cookies have been displayed. The variety is outstanding; the flavors, divine. Christy says each woman fills her container with two of each kind of cookie to take home. Christy puts her plastic container, loaded down with cookies, into the freezer. When company comes, she has instant dessert on hand.

At other cookie exchanges, each participant is expected to bring six or eight dozen favorite holiday sweets. That way everyone can take home a full dozen or more of each variety and assemble cookie assortments to package up in gift tins for school bus drivers, piano teachers, office colleagues, or building staff — and, of course, for neighbors.

CREAMY ICING

makes ³/₄ cup

2 cups confectioners' sugar
2 tablespoons melted butter
1 teaspoon vanilla extract
2 tablespoons heavy cream
Food coloring, optional

Sift the sugar into a large bowl ½ cup at a time. Add the melted butter, vanilla, and cream. Add the food coloring, if using, and with an electric hand mixer on medium speed, beat until the mixture is creamy and spreadable. It should have the consistency of peanut butter. Add a bit more cream if necessary.

BRYSELL COOKIES

makes about 5 dozen cookies

Laurie Gabriel has been part of a cookie exchange in southern New Hampshire for more than fifteen years, and this is her favorite contribution. It is a great refrigerator cookie; simply roll the logs with sprinkles, wrap them tightly in plastic wrap, and refrigerate or freeze them until it's time to bake. You can slice them right from the freezer, but add 2 to 3 minutes to the baking time.

1 pound (4 sticks) butter

1 cup confectioners' sugar

1 teaspoon vanilla extract

3 cups all-purpose flour

Red and green sprinkles

Cream the butter, sugar, and vanilla in a large mixing bowl. Add the flour, and mix well. Divide the dough into 4 equal portions, and form each portion into a log 1 inch in diameter. Roll 2 logs in the red sprinkles and 2 in the green sprinkles, pressing them onto the sides. Chill the logs for an hour.

Preheat the oven to 350°F. Cut the rolls into ½-inch-thick slices, and place the slices on ungreased cookie sheets. Bake until the cookies are golden, 8 to 10 minutes. Cool the cookies on wire racks.

HOLIDAY SPICE COOKIES

makes about fifty 3-inch cookies

You can make this dough up to three weeks in advance.

4 cups all-purpose flour

1$\frac{1}{2}$ teaspoons ground cinnamon

1 teaspoon ground ginger

$\frac{1}{2}$ teaspoon ground nutmeg

$\frac{1}{2}$ teaspoon salt

$\frac{1}{4}$ teaspoon ground allspice

$\frac{1}{4}$ teaspoon ground cloves

1$\frac{1}{2}$ cups butter at room temperature

1 cup granulated sugar

1 large egg

1 teaspoon vanilla extract

Preheat the oven to 375°F.

In a large bowl mix the flour, cinnamon, ginger, nutmeg, salt, allspice, and cloves until blended. With an electric mixer blend together the butter and sugar until light and fluffy. Beat in the egg and vanilla. Reduce the mixer speed to low and gradually add the flour mixture, beating until well blended. Divide the dough in thirds. Shape each into a ball and flatten to a 1-inch-thick round. Wrap in plastic wrap and refrigerate 1 hour or until firm enough to roll.

On a lightly floured surface, roll one third of the dough at a time to ¼-inch thickness (keep the remainder refrigerated). Cut the dough in shapes with floured cookie cutters. Place 1 inch apart on ungreased cookie sheets. (Chill and reroll scraps.)

Bake the cookies for about 12 minutes or until they are golden on the undersides and the edges are just starting to brown. Cool completely on the cookie sheet on a wire rack. Ice and decorate as desired.

PEANUT BUTTER COOKIES

makes about 6 dozen small cookies

Suburban childhoods are fueled by peanut butter cookies, an American tradition worth preserving.

1¼ cups flour

½ teaspoon salt

½ teaspoon baking soda

¼ pound (1 stick) butter, softened

½ cup peanut butter

½ cup granulated sugar

½ cup packed brown sugar

1 large egg

½ teaspoon vanilla extract

Preheat the oven to 350°F.

Sift together the flour, salt, and baking soda, and set them aside.

In a mixing bowl, combine the butter and peanut butter, and beat until they're creamy. Beat in the sugars; then beat in the egg and vanilla.

Add the dry ingredients, and beat well. The mixture should be just stiff enough to hold its shape when you scoop it up with a spoon. If it is too soft, stir in a little more flour (no more than ¼ cup should be needed).

Arrange teaspoonfuls of dough on an ungreased baking sheet. Dip the tines of a fork in flour and use the back of the fork to press a crosshatch pattern into the top of each cookie.

Bake the cookies until they're golden, about 10 minutes. Transfer the cookies to wire racks to cool.

CABA COOBA BALLS

makes 4 dozen cookies

These have been in Sue Benjamin's family for generations and are loved by all.

- ¹/₂ pound (2 sticks) butter, softened
- ¹/₄ cup packed brown sugar
- ¹/₄ cup granulated sugar
- 1 tablespoon vanilla extract
- 1 cup chopped almonds, toasted and cooled
- 12 ounces chocolate chips
- 2 cups sifted flour
- Confectioners' sugar

Preheat the oven to 350°F.

In a mixer bowl, combine the butter and sugars, and cream them together until fluffy. Beat in the vanilla, then stir in the almonds and chocolate chips. Add the flour, and knead the dough with your fingers until the flour is incorporated. Roll the dough into 1-inch balls, and place them on ungreased cookie sheets.

Bake the cookies for 15 minutes. Cool them slightly on the baking sheet; then roll them in confectioners' sugar. Cool the cookies completely, and store them in an airtight tin.

OATMEAL-PECAN SHORTBREAD

shortbread

makes 20 wedges

Really good and really easy! The dough may be made up to three days before baking.

$^2/_3$ cup butter, softened

$^1/_2$ cup sugar

1 teaspoon vanilla extract

1$^1/_2$ cups all-purpose flour

$^1/_4$ cup finely chopped pecans

$^1/_4$ cup quick-cooking oats

20 pecan halves

Preheat the oven to 300°F; spray a 9-inch fluted tart pan with a removable bottom with nonstick cooking spray.

In a large bowl, beat the butter, sugar, and vanilla at medium speed, until light and fluffy; at low speed, gradually beat in the flour until thoroughly blended and smooth. Stir in the chopped pecans and oats.

Pat the dough into the prepared pan in an even layer. Lightly score the top into 20 wedges with the dull edge of a knife. Press 1 pecan half into the wide end of each scored wedge.

Bake until the shortbread is evenly browned, about 45 to 55 minutes. Cool the shortbread in the pan on a wire rack for 30 minutes, until only slightly warm. Remove the sides of the pan. Using a sharp knife, cut the shortbread along the score marks into wedges. Cool the wedges completely on the rack. Store the shortbread in a tightly covered container at room temperature for up to 1 week.

FARRIS FAMILY FESTIVE FUDGE

makes 18 pieces

Kathie and Jeff Farris have begun a tradition with their two young daughters. Every Christmas they make many batches of fudge and package them up, complete with a little logo they made on their home computer and a list of ingredients: love, health, and happiness. They bundle up the girls and deliver a package to each neighbor.

3 cups sugar

$\frac{1}{8}$ teaspoon salt

$\frac{2}{3}$ cup Hershey's cocoa

$1\frac{1}{2}$ cups milk

4 tablespoons butter

2 teaspoons vanilla extract

Combine the sugar, salt, cocoa, and milk in a saucepan, and cook, stirring, until the sugar melts. Continue to cook slowly, without stirring, to the soft-ball stage, 236°F on a candy thermometer.

Remove the fudge from the heat. Add the butter, but do not stir. Set the fudge aside to cool. When the pan is cool enough that you can hold your hand on the bottom, add the vanilla, and beat the fudge until it is no longer shiny, but is thick and creamy. Quickly pour it into a large buttered loaf pan, and mark in squares to make 18 large pieces.

VARIATION

You can add 1 cup of chopped nuts or 12 marshmallows cut into pieces with wet scissors. Stir them in just before turning the fudge into the loaf pan.

caroling

Many neighborhoods gather for Christmas caroling. There are a few different ways to go. Traditional caroling has folks gathering at one spot and moving from house to house singing songs, eventually ending up at the host's home for hot cider and desserts. One neighborhood incorporates caroling with the progressive dinner format. About sixty-five people, including out-of-town relatives and college students back home on vacation, gather at the appetizer house. They all head out caroling from there and end up at the dinner house, where the potluck meal waits.

If you want to have a real crowd singing, consider gathering in one spot and letting everyone know to come by. I know of one neighborhood where this is such a long-standing tradition that all the carolers sport uniforms of red scarves and plaid hats. Regardless of where you gather outside, when it's time to come in, the food and drink should be festive and warming.

MINTED BARK

makes 10 servings

Wrap this gracious holiday treat in pretty foil or cellophane bags for hostess gifts. A clean takeout container tied with ribbon is another fun packaging idea.

1 cup peppermint candies

12 ounces white chocolate, chopped

8 ounces semisweet chocolate, chopped

$1/4$ teaspoon peppermint extract

Line a baking sheet with parchment paper.

Put the peppermint candies in a food processor, and pulse until they're finely chopped.

Melt the chocolates separately over gently simmering water. Add the peppermint extract to the white chocolate with ½ cup of the ground peppermint candy. Stir the remaining candy into the dark chocolate.

Pour the white chocolate onto the parchment paper in 3 wide, thin strips, leaving room between each strip.

Next, pour the dark chocolate into 2 strips between the white strips. Drag a knife crosswise through the white and dark chocolate to create a swirled, marbled effect.

Gently shake the pan, and tap the bottom firmly until all air bubbles are cleared from the chocolate mixtures.

When the mixture is cool and slightly firm to the touch, cover and refrigerate it until it's hardened. Break the candy into bite-size pieces, and store it in a cool place.

SCENTED ORNAMENTS

Nothing will put you in the holiday spirit more than making (or receiving) these aromatic decorations. Tie them onto the tree or on packages. It's a great project for kids too young to bake. Middle Eastern stores or warehouse clubs are good places to buy inexpensive bulk spices like cinnamon.

$^3/_4$ cup cinnamon

1 tablespoon allspice

2 tablespoons cloves

1 tablespoon nutmeg

1 cup applesauce

Mix all the ingredients in a bowl, working the dough well. If the mixture is too moist, add more cinnamon. Roll it out onto a waxed-paper-covered cookie sheet. Use seasonal cookie cutters to cut the dough into shapes. Create holes in each ornament for hanging by using straws, wooden skewers, or toothpicks to pierce the dough.

Allow the ornaments to air-dry for 4 to 5 days.

Making the Holidays Count

Many philanthropic and relief organizations work hard to provide holiday gifts and meals for underprivileged children and families. One neighborhood, committed to bringing more meaning to the holidays, worked with the Salvation Army to "adopt" two families for Christmas. Although anonymous, the neighborhood knew the ages of the kids and a little something about the parents. Collectively the neighborhood made certain that every member had plenty of gifts to open and a glorious Christmas dinner.

SPIKED EGGNOG

spiked eggnog

makes 16 to 20 servings

This is high-test nog, so make sure your guests know that it's spiked. For the children, substitute apple juice for bourbon and cognac.

12 large eggs

1 cup sugar

1 cup bourbon

1 cup cognac

$^1/_2$ teaspoon salt

3 pints heavy cream

$^1/_2$ teaspoon grated nutmeg

Separate the eggs. In an electric mixer, beat the egg yolks with the sugar until they're slightly thickened and a pale yellow.

Slowly add the bourbon and cognac, and beat at slow speed. Chill the mixture, covered, for several hours.

An hour before serving the eggnog, add the salt to the egg whites, and beat until they're almost stiff, or until the beaten whites form a peak that bends slightly.

In another bowl, whip the cream until it's stiff. Fold the whipped cream into the chilled yolk mixture; then fold in the beaten egg whites. Chill for 1 hour.

When you're ready to serve, put the eggnog into a chilled bowl, and sprinkle it with freshly grated nutmeg.

DEB LECHNER'S WINE MULL

makes 20 (4-ounce) servings

This recipe has been in Deb's family for over thirty years, and her neighbors look forward to it when December rolls around.

1 cup sugar

15 whole cloves

1 cinnamon stick

5 star anise

Grated zest of $1/2$ lemon

3 cups water

2 (750-ml) bottles dry red table wine

Simmer the sugar, cloves, cinnamon stick, anise, lemon zest, and water for 15 minutes in a large saucepan. If you prefer, you can strain the mixture at this point, but the spices will look pretty floating in the wine.

Add the wine, and heat it, but do not boil. Serve this drink warm and in mugs.

PEAR BREAD PUDDING

pear bread pudding

makes 10 to 12 servings

Use good bread and delectable Comice pears if they're available—it makes a fine dessert that much better.

3 large pears, preferably Comice, peeled, cored, and sliced

1/2 cup sugar

1 cup dry red wine

Scant 1/2 teaspoon ground cinnamon

Scant 1/2 teaspoon ground nutmeg

4 cups dry bread cubes

custard

2 cups whole milk

1/2 cup sugar

1 teaspoon vanilla extract

Pinch of salt

5 large eggs, beaten

Scant 1/2 teaspoon ground cinnamon

Scant 1/2 teaspoon ground nutmeg

1/2 cup dark rum

In a saucepan, simmer the pears, sugar, wine, cinnamon, and nutmeg. Remove the pan from the heat when the syrup has thickened and barely covers the pears, about 10 minutes. Set the pears aside while you make the custard.

Heat the 2 cups of milk to just under a boil. Add 1/2 cup sugar and the vanilla and salt. Remove the milk mixture from the heat and beat it very gradually into the beaten eggs. Add the cinnamon, nutmeg, and rum, and mix well.

Butter a 9 × 13–inch baking dish. Put the bread cubes in it, and add the custard. Press down on the bread cubes to absorb the custard. Let it soak for about 15 minutes. Preheat the oven to 325°F.

Place the baking dish in a larger pan of hot water, and bake, uncovered, for 20 minutes. Remove the dish from the oven and spread the pear mixture over the custard. Return it to the oven for 20 more minutes, being careful not to overcook.

Serve the pudding warm with softly whipped cream that's lightly sweetened with confectioners' sugar and ½ teaspoon of vanilla, or serve it plain. Have the leftovers for breakfast!

You Sleigh Me!

In Wildwood, Maine, Santa spends the night before Christmas on the back of a pickup truck. Each Christmas Eve a very large sleigh is pulled from one neighbor's garage and hoisted onto an open-bed pickup. Santa cruises the neighborhood tossing candies to all the young children. One year he rode in a Boston Whaler powerboat strapped on a trailer.

EDIBLE SUGARED FRUIT

You don't have to be a professional caterer to create an edible centerpiece. Arrange the sugared fruit on a cake stand, or stacked cake stands, or an epergne, if you have one, in the middle of your buffet table. It's both edible and for show.

Powdered egg whites

Water, to reconstitute eggs

Champagne grapes, small pears, or lady apples

Granulated sugar

Mix the egg whites with a little water to form a thin, fluid paste. Paint selected fruits and sprinkle them with sugar. Let the sugar set for 1 hour before arranging the fruit decoratively on a centerpiece.

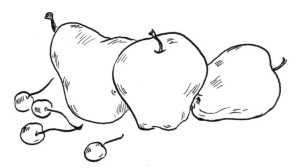

FRUITED CHEESE LOG

makes 24 servings as an appetizer

A nice, sweet touch for an autumn hors d'oeuvre.

1 (8-ounce) package cream cheese, softened

$^1/_2$ pound Cheddar cheese, shredded

2 tablespoons honey

2 tablespoons dry sherry

1 teaspoon curry powder

2 chopped scallions

$^1/_4$ cup chopped dried apricots

$^1/_4$ cup chopped dried apples

2 tablespoons coarsely chopped raisins

2 tablespoons chopped dates

$^1/_2$ cup chopped nuts

Crackers, for serving

In a medium bowl or food processor, combine the cream cheese, Cheddar, honey, sherry, and curry powder. Blend until the ingredients are well mixed. Stir in the scallions and dried fruits by hand.

Form the mixture into a log about 1½ inches in diameter, and roll it in the chopped nuts. Wrap the log tightly in plastic wrap, and refrigerate it from 2 hours to 4 days before serving time. Serve the appetizer with crackers.

FRUIT DIP

fruit dip

makes 3 cups

Is it dessert? Is it a dip? You decide. I just know it's delicious and kids can't get enough.

1 (16-ounce) jar marshmallow cream

1 (8-ounce) package cream cheese, softened

8 cups strawberries, seedless grapes,
  or apple or pear slices

1 cup pretzel nuggets

Whip together marshmallow cream and cream cheese until they're well mixed. Serve Fruit Dip with several types of fruit and pretzels.

keep them on their toes

Fred Wilkenson of Charlotte, North Carolina, knows he's a troublemaker. He's the kind of guy who'll show up to a formal event in loud plaid pants and a cowboy hat. His five thousand colored Christmas lights don't really acknowledge the neighborhood memo that encourages white twinkle lights. About eight years ago Fred gave a new twist to the annual holiday party—a potluck hors d'oeuvres gathering that he felt had become a bit stale. An hour before the party, he got out the good crystal bowl. He plopped a can of Spam on a dry rice cake and loaded it with colorful toothpicks and surrounded it with saltines. It was a hit. No one ate it, but everyone talked about it for days. Each year, Fred comes up with a new way to ensure that a Spam dish arrives at the party anonymously. Some of the best creations included Stonehedge Spam and 2000 and Spam. Both were sculptures to be envied (but not eaten!).

Recently, Fred has escalated the challenge with edible Spam creations. The Spam Chocolate Torte and Spam-in-a-Blanket are two of his recent successes.

ring in the new

Many neighborhoods throw New Year's Eve parties. One clever idea is to hire the older kids as baby-sitters and turn one house into the Baby-sitter's Club, while the adults have their own party in a home nearby. This way kids can start at the adult party, but as they get tired they can go over and join the sleeping-bag crowd at the Baby-sitter's Club.

Debbie Lechner said that to make one New Year's Eve special, she and her neighbors brought out their photo albums and compared pictures of how much the block had changed in the last fourteen years. (Out of sixteen houses, eight have their original owners.) They made a time capsule with funny predictions about neighbors and the block. The funniest guesses were the ones from the kids.

Another idea is to welcome the new year by bringing everyone together for a casual open house meal on New Year's Day. Professional football on TV and perhaps touch football in the nearby park are de rigueur. Make it potluck, and make it memorable. Here are some fun party games that might be just right for your crowd:

- Charades
- Football betting pool
- A neighborhood trivia sheet
- Musical clues—I went to a party where we each had to wear a clue to a popular song. It took all afternoon to figure out why the host, Pinky Fowler, was wearing a falsie on her head with a small plastic branch. I will never forget the song—"Titwillow."

ANGELS ON HORSEBACK

A traditional oyster appetizer. Pass these around while they're nice and hot, and watch 'em disappear!

12 bacon slices, cut in half

1 pint small shucked oysters, drained

$1/2$ teaspoon salt

$1/8$ teaspoon pepper

$1/8$ teaspoon paprika

2 tablespoons chopped parsley

Preheat the oven to 450°F. Fit a small baking rack into a baking pan, and spritz the rack with vegetable cooking spray.

On a clean surface, lay out the bacon slice halves, and top each with an oyster. (Cut the oysters into pieces if they're too large.) Season the oysters with salt, pepper, paprika, and parsley. Roll the bacon around the oysters, and secure them with wooden toothpicks.

Arrange the wrapped oysters on the rack, and bake them until the bacon is crisp, about 10 minutes. Serve this appetizer immediately.

CHARD-STUFFED PROSCIUTTO ROLLS

makes 18 roll-ups

Swiss chard is a wonderful and underused cold-weather vegetable. It's a good match for the sophisticated Italian flavors of prosciutto and balsamic vinegar.

- 3 tablespoons extra virgin olive oil
- 1 bunch of red or green Swiss chard leaves (or spinach, escarole, or mustard greens), stemmed and coarsely chopped (about 6 cups)
- 4 garlic cloves, minced (2 teaspoons)
- 2 tablespoons balsamic vinegar
- 1/4 teaspoon salt
- 1/8 teaspoon freshly ground pepper
- 1/2 pound very thinly sliced prosciutto or ham (18 slices)

In a large nonreactive skillet, heat the olive oil over medium heat. Add the greens and cook, tossing, until they're wilted, about 1 to 2 minutes. Stir in the garlic, vinegar, salt, and pepper. Cook until the greens are just tender, about 1 minute. Remove them from the heat.

Lay the prosciutto or ham slices on a work surface. Place a generous tablespoon of greens at one end of each slice, and roll the slice into a tight cylinder, leaving some of the green protruding. Transfer the rolls to a serving tray; cover, and refrigerate them for up to 8 hours. Serve the roll-ups at room temperature or slightly chilled.

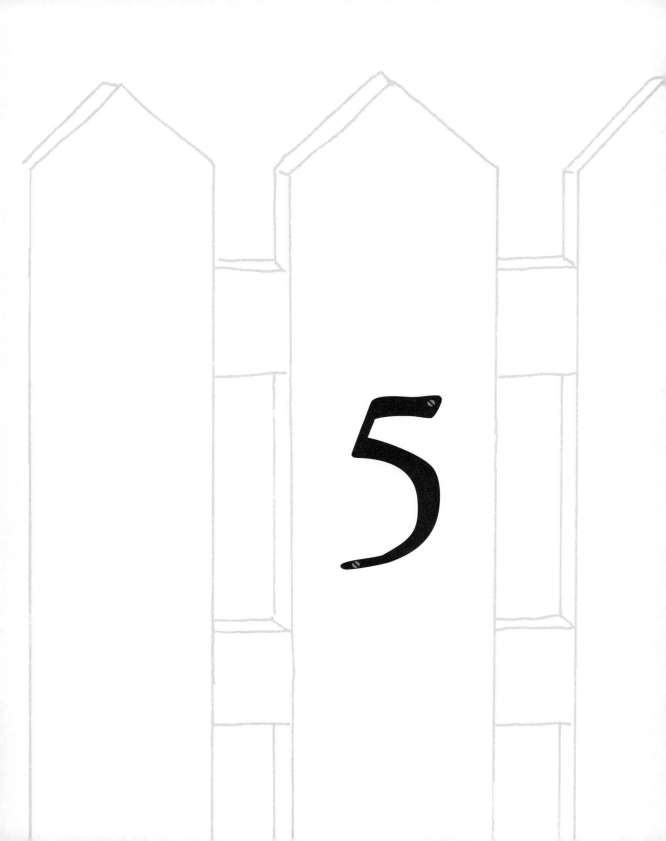

good times and bad

One of the most important rewards of belonging to a neighborhood is getting the opportunity to help and be helped in the good times and the tough times. At some time every neighborhood will be touched by loss and suffering, often without warning. It isn't always easy for people to know when someone needs assistance, and it is even harder to know how to ask for it. I think people, in general, truly feel relief when they get real help. Even happy events, like the birth of a new child, can bring challenges that require otherwise self-sufficient, competent people to lean gratefully on concerned friends.

Comfort Meals

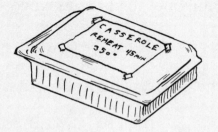

Be the neighbor people call. One of the very best reasons to know your neighbors is so that you have people to count on in an emergency—big or small. Our neighbor Pete Mitchell has rescued our house so many times, it's embarrassing. He handled the police when our home was burglarized while we were on vacation and helped a baby-sitter break into the house when she had locked herself out.

Be prepared to do the right thing, and conduct yourself in such a way that neighbors will know they can count on you.

- Offer to watch out for a neighbor's house and water their plants while they're on vacation.
- Be willing to baby-sit a child or pet when something sudden comes up.
- Let neighbors know if you saw something suspicious at their house.
- Toss the newspaper up on the porch.

the tough times

When a hockey injury sent a neighbor of ours to the hospital right before Christmas, no one expected the X-ray to show he had a liver tumor. Suddenly a busy family of five needed to put everything on hold to care for Andy. Weeks of hospital stays and a slow recovery took their toll on everyone, but neighbors did much to ease the strain. From warm meals delivered each day to car pools for the kids, folks from blocks away stepped up to the plate.

It is not easy to know what to do for a family in need. It's tempting to drop a casserole at the back door and be done with it, but while hot meals are certainly welcome, lots more may be required. Sudden illnesses or accidents demand so much of a family, they may not be able to

- Shovel the walk of a neighbor who you know won't be home until later.
- Call an older couple just to say hello.
- Make a big pot of soup. Take some in a plastic, throwaway container to that single person on your block who works such long hours.

Sharing your time, your energy, and some of your stuff is what you can do. From there, the creativity of your generosity will begin to grow.

Providing hot meals to a household in need is the essence of what neighborhood living is all about. In this chapter you'll find comfort meals that transport well and offer the kind of familiar dishes that families will appreciate in good times and bad. Best of all, you'll discover that stirring up a pot of something sustaining—and seeing the grateful look on the recipient's face—really does make *you* feel a lot better, too!

really communicate their needs in the beginning. Neighbors should refrain from calling the house; instead, a single neighbor should step up to be the point person, coordinating the efforts of those who want to help out. That person should stay in touch with the family, and make clear that there are loads of people ready to do tasks small and large. The point person can also turn to neighbors to set up an immediate plan to cover the family with meals for a week or longer, and let the family know it's coming with a note or brief message.

If possible, bring meals that don't require anything more than reheating and a couple of dishes to return. (There are now disposable serving dishes if you really want to make life simple for everybody.)

MAKE-AHEAD BEEF BOURGUIGNON

makes 3 batches, each serving 4

Most stews are better if you make them ahead and reheat them. I've taken that principle one step further. I make the meat portion of this recipe and divide it into three freezer bags. When I need an instant hearty meal, I defrost one bag, add the vegetables, and heat it through. Keep the meat portion frozen for up to 3 months.

$1/2$ pound bacon, chopped into small pieces

3 pounds beef chuck, cut into 1-inch cubes

1 cup chopped onions

Salt and pepper to taste

3 tablespoons unbleached all-purpose flour

3 cups red wine (burgundy, if you have it)

3 cups beef broth

2 tablespoons tomato paste

1 tablespoon fresh rosemary (or 1 teaspoon dried)

for each frozen bag, when you're ready to serve it, you will add

1 (12-ounce) bag frozen peas

2 diced carrots, cooked

$1/4$ cup fresh parsley

Preheat the oven to 350°F.

In a heavy casserole, cook the bacon until it's crisp. Remove it with a slotted spoon, and drain it on a paper towel. Pour off and discard all except 1 tablespoon of the bacon fat.

Over medium heat, brown the beef cubes in the bacon fat on all sides, working in batches. Return the beef cubes to the pot, add the onions, and sprinkle the meat with the salt and pepper and the flour. Cook the mixture over high heat, stirring constantly for about 5 minutes.

Add the wine, beef broth, tomato paste, rosemary, and the cooked bacon, and bring the mixture to a boil. Cover the dish, and place it in the oven.

Bake until the meat is tender, about 2 hours. Let the mixture cool until just warm to the touch. Label and date 3 freezer bags, and divide the stew evenly among them.

To serve, defrost one of the meat packages just enough to transfer the frozen block to a casserole dish. Heat very slowly. Add the peas and carrots; then add the parsley. If it's too thick, add a little beef broth. Serve the stew over egg noodles.

neighborly ways

Once you begin to think as a neighbor, the opportunities to be one are all around you. Step out of your home, out of your family demands, and stay tuned in.

- Share tools
- Lend car seats
- Pass along a swing set
- Walk along both sides of the street

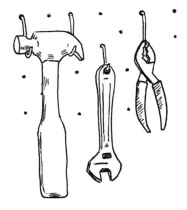

STUFFED PORK LOIN

Fruit and pork is always a terrific combination, and this impressive roast is no exception. This will serve four people amply with plenty of leftovers. Send along a container of steamed rice or couscous.

2 large tart apples

12 pitted prunes

1 (4½- to 5-pound) boned pork loin (not too thick), opened flat

Salt and pepper

Vegetable oil

¾ cup heavy cream

¾ cup dry white wine

3 tablespoons currant jelly

Preheat the oven to 350°F.

Cut up the apples and prunes, and arrange them down the center of the loin. Season with salt and pepper. Roll the roast and tie it; then rub the outside with vegetable oil.

Brown the loin under the broiler, turning it to brown all sides evenly.

Place the loin in an ovenproof casserole. Add the cream, wine, and jelly to the pan, cover it, and bake until the meat shows no resistance when cut with a knife, about 1½ hours.

Remove the loin from the casserole, and place it in a covered pan or dish to keep it warm while you make the gravy.

Skim the fat from the pan liquid. Place the casserole over medium heat, and reduce the liquid to 1 cup, stirring until the mixture is smooth. The mixture may be thickened further, if you like, with butter and flour (see below). Season the gravy to taste with salt and pepper.

Slice the tenderloin ¼ inch thick, and serve it with gravy on the side. To transport the meal, wrap the tenderloin tightly in foil, and pack the gravy in a jar or plastic container.

If you like your gravy thicker, you can stir in small bits of butter masked together with an equal amount of flour. Add ½ teaspoon at a time, and cook for 1 minute or so before thickening further.

NEVER-FAIL BAKED RICE

makes 8 servings

Your rice can cook in the oven, undisturbed, while you attend to other things.

2 cups rice

1 teaspoon salt

4 cups boiling water

4 tablespoons butter

Chopped parsley

Preheat the oven to 350°F.

Put the rice in a 1½-quart baking dish. Add the salt and boiling water. Stir, cover, and bake the rice for 35 to 40 minutes, or until the rice is tender.

Stir in the butter and chopped parsley, and serve timmediately.

being neighborly

- One winter we seemed to get more snow than we had places to put it. After one particularly bad dumping, my husband and I were shoveling away and noticed that there were no tracks or evidence of movement across the street. An older couple lived in the house, and the husband often traveled for work. When we were done shoveling our driveway, we went across the street and shoveled them out. It was hard work and took some time, but it seemed the right thing to do. Four weeks later, a lovely woven basket loaded with African violets arrived at our door. The note said, "I didn't learn until yesterday who shoveled us out. Thank you!"

- In one very generous neighborhood, tools are shared regularly. Ed has the tall stepladder, Bob has the stud finder and battery charger, Tom has anything you need to fix a car. They also think like neighbors for bigger items; when they rent a lawn plugger, they pass it around the block, and everyone who uses it puts in five dollars. Recently, when one neighbor bought brown paint for his mailbox post, he passed it down the block with a brush wrapped in plastic wrap so everyone could paint their posts.

- Even when they're away, Debbie Lechner's family can count on their neighbors. Recently, when they were camping, the supply line to their toilet at home burst and pumped three feet of water through the first floor of their home. One neighbor saw the water coming from under the garage door and used an extra key to get in and turn off the water. Then two families used a Shop-Vac to pump out as much water as they could, while two more families ferried the furniture to safety. Without the neighbors' help, the Lechners might have lost many of their possessions. Several weeks later, they had a big pizza and beer party in the backyard for all the people who had rescued their home.

- One spring morning, very early, we saw a woman in a bathrobe with a worried look sweeping the street not far from us. Apparently a car had driven by and struck the glass recycling box, spilling broken glass everywhere. It wasn't her box, it was her neighbor's. We went and got our broom and pitched in.

- When the Martinage home in upstate New York was badly damaged by fire, their neighbors took the family in and sheltered them for a month while things were under repair.

- In another upstate New York community, a neighbor with a playing field adjacent to his home spends hours every week keeping the field in shape so that kids can play football and baseball there—and their parents will know where they are.

- Feeling pressed for time on weeknights? Try sharing cooking duties with a neighbor. Make a double batch of dinner, and deliver it to your partner one night a week so each of you gets a day off to do things with your children after school or work a half hour later.

- The shaft of an old shovel broke in half while my husband was doing some spring planting. He put the busted shovel out in the alley and leaned it against the garbage cans for the next day's trash. About two weeks later, Nick Sievers from two houses down came by with the shovel and presented it to Todd. He had replaced the shaft, sharpened the blade, and added a handle.

- Whenever someone buys a new car in a large cul-de-sac I know about, they must take possession and hang from their rearview mirror—with pride—the neighborhood set of oversize, soft fuzzy dice.

- Plenty of neighborhoods know how to pitch in when big jobs need to be done. In one area, an entire roof went up on a garage over the weekend thanks to a few phone calls and the promise of a meal. Ten guys, tools in hand, worked together to get it done.

- If your garden is an abundant one, share extra fruits and vegetables with older neighbors who can't garden anymore.

- Keep your sense of humor. Generosity can sometimes backfire. Randy Sable was snowblowing his sidewalks and wanted to do the same for his neighbors. He was about half done when he ran over the extension cord for the Christmas lights at the Mitchells' house. Randy fixed the extension cord, finished the job, and then crossed the street to plow the Pearces' walk. As Randy made his way up the path to the front door, he saw the homeowner in the window frantically waving his arms just as he cut the power to their outdoor Christmas lights. It's hard to believe, but Randy had managed to run over two extension cords during a single act of kindness.

MOLLY O'BRIEN'S HOT CHICKEN SALAD

makes 8 servings

Like me, Molly has relied on her mom for favorite recipes. Here is one she returns to time and again.

2½ cups cubed cooked chicken breast

1 (8-ounce) can sliced water chestnuts, drained

1 (8-ounce) jar sliced pimientos, drained

½ cup slivered almonds, toasted in a nonstick skillet until golden (about 3 minutes)

1 (8-ounce) can sliced mushrooms, drained

1½ cups mayonnaise

2 tablespoons fresh lemon juice

1 (8-ounce) bag grated Cheddar cheese

1 (8-ounce) can French onion rings

Preheat the oven to 350°F.

In a mixing bowl, thoroughly combine the chicken, water chestnuts, pimientos, toasted almonds, mushrooms, mayonnaise, and lemon juice. Transfer the mixture to a 9 × 13–inch baking dish. Top the salad with the cheese and onion rings. Cover it with aluminum foil.

Bake the salad for about 20 minutes; then remove the foil and bake until it's bubbly, about 5 more minutes, being careful not to burn the onion rings.

DORIS TIPPENS' CHICKEN

3/03 really good!

chicken

makes 8 to 10 servings

One of my mom's best friends prepared this dish regularly. What makes it so outstanding, besides the great flavors, is that you don't have to bother browning the chicken. Make a pot of rice, and pour the pan juices over it for an extra side dish.

1 cup dry red wine

$^1/_4$ cup soy sauce

$^1/_4$ cup vegetable oil

2 tablespoons water

1 garlic clove, smashed

1 teaspoon ground ginger

$^1/_4$ teaspoon dried oregano

2 packed tablespoons brown sugar

2 (2- to 3-pound) chickens, cut into serving pieces

Combine all the ingredients but the chicken in a sealable plastic bag or large bowl, and mix them well. Add the chicken, and marinate it in the refrigerator for at least 6 hours, or overnight.

Preheat the oven to 375°F.

Arrange the chicken pieces in a single layer in a 9 × 13–inch baking dish. Pour the marinade over the chicken, and bake until it's tender, about 1¼ hours.

the birth of a baby

The anticipation of a new arrival in the family can be almost as exciting for neighbors as for the family itself. It brings generations together, and the sight of tiny fingers and toes can melt even the most jaded characters. Many neighborhoods have a standing chain that is activated any time a family gets a new member. Once any helping parents or siblings have gone home, two weeks of hot meals arrive like clockwork, with one household given Tuesday, another Wednesday, and so on. Since leftovers are inevitable, every third day is skipped.

Other ideas for a baby's arrival might include the following:

- Before the baby is born, send a note with an offer to baby-sit any older siblings.

- One neighborhood I know of plants a tree for every new baby.

- Don't forget that adoptive parents can use a helping hand, too.

- Don't offer *any* parenting advice unless asked.

- Offer to do a grocery run or the laundry.

- Drop off some rented movies with a note that says you'll pick them up the day they're due back.

- After six weeks, when any new mom is exhausted but ready for adult conversation, call ahead to make a date to come over for lunch. Pack up a laundry basket with everything for a special lunch. Arrive on time, and don't stay longer than one hour. Take everything with you from the lunch, but leave behind a dinner for the family and a few great mindless magazines.

My sister was pregnant with her first child shortly after she moved to Jersey City, New Jersey. A neighbor she had never met before stopped her on the sidewalk to ask if she had bought any baby gear. Days later the neighbor arrived with a swing chair, high chair, and car seat. How generous! If you do accept items from neighbors, find out if the item is a loaner that should be returned, or if it is an item they no longer want or need. If you are borrowing something, be it a tool or a bassinet, return it in good shape and in a timely manner.

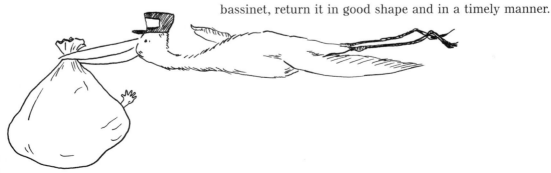

MOM'S CURRY CHICKEN SOUP

makes 6 to 8 servings

My mom began making this soup after watching Julia Child prepare something similar on TV in the late sixties. Julia added heavy cream, which my mom doesn't use, and my mom uses convenient frozen veggies. She always has a quart in the freezer just in case there's a neighbor in need (or my dad is hungry).

4 tablespoons (½ stick) butter

½ cup chopped onion

2 tablespoons curry powder

½ cup flour

6 cups chicken broth

1 (16-ounce) bag frozen mixed carrots and peas

1 cup chopped parsnips or turnips

2 cups diced cooked chicken

Melt the butter in a large 3- to 4-quart, heavy-bottomed pot. Add the onions, and sauté until they are translucent, 5 or 6 minutes. Add the curry, and stir another 1 minute over low heat. Add the flour, and stir for 2 minutes. Let this cool just a bit. (This roux helps thicken the soup.)

Slowly whisk in the chicken broth, and bring it to a simmer. The soup should now be pleasantly thick.

Following the package instructions, microwave the frozen carrots and peas, and add them to the soup. Steam the parsnips until they are tender, and add them to the soup, along with the chicken. Continue to simmer for another 30 minutes.

DOC'S FAVORITE SHEPHERD'S PIE

Kate, the busy wife of a country doctor and the mother of six, found out her family considered this fantastic Sunday fare. If Doc had to go deliver a baby, this dish was even better rewarmed when he finally got home. It's Kate's choice when a neighbor needs a meal.

2 tablespoons vegetable oil

1 medium onion, chopped (³/₄ cup)

2 pounds lean ground beef or chuck

1 (8-ounce) can tomato paste

¹/₂ teaspoon minced garlic (1 clove)

Salt and black pepper to taste

2 cups frozen French-cut green beans

2 large eggs

8 -serving portion of seasoned, prepared instant mashed potatoes

¹/₄ cup grated Parmesan cheese

Heat the oil in a heavy skillet. Add the onion and ground meat, and cook until the meat is no longer pink, breaking up the chunks with a wooden spoon. Drain off any fat.

Stir in the tomato paste, garlic, and a small tomato paste can of water. Cook and stir the mixture for about 2 minutes. It should be moist, but not soupy. If necessary, cook a bit longer to evaporate some of the liquid. Taste and season the casserole as desired with the salt and pepper. Transfer it to an oiled 2-quart casserole and stir in the frozen green beans.

Preheat the oven to 375°F. Using a mixer, add the eggs to the mashed potatoes, one at a time, beating well after each addition. Beat in the Parmesan cheese.

Spread the potato mixture over the meat, covering the entire casserole. Bake until the potatoes are golden brown, about 30 minutes.

midnight giggles

Kirsten Lambert puts together a baby gift basket of newborn-size disposable diapers with strict instructions that the diapers are to be used only after midnight. Each diaper contains a slip of paper with a little late-night humor—who couldn't use a grin at that hour? Here are some of the inscriptions.

- In sixteen years you'll be up at this time waiting for him to come home.
- Remember, the diaper goes on the end that is quiet. The pacifier goes in the loud side.
- So, what's on TV this early in the morning?
- "There are only two reasons to sit in the back row of an airplane: either you have diarrhea, or you're anxious to meet people who do."—Henry Kissinger
- "Women complain about premenstrual syndrome, but I think of it as the only time of the month that I can be myself."—Roseanne
- www.sleep.com

When Wendy Kaiser became a new mom, she learned from her doorman that fourteen other babies had been born in her building that same year! She organized an informal gathering in the function room of her building. "I decided this would be a great way for all the parents and babies to meet. So often, living in a big building like mine, you come home, get on the elevator, get off on your floor—and don't really see anyone else!"

LAMB STEW WITH CANNELLINI BEANS

lamb stew

Here's a one-dish meal that calls for nothing more than crispy bread, a robust red wine, and sliced oranges drizzled with olive oil and sage to complete.

3	tablespoons olive oil
3½	pounds lamb shoulder
1½	pounds cubed lamb stew meat
⅔	cup all-purpose flour
2½	cups chopped onion
1	teaspoon dried sage
1	cup dry white wine
	Salt and pepper to taste
2	teaspoons tomato paste
1	cup beef broth
2	(19-ounce) cans cannellini beans, drained
2	teaspoons minced garlic (4 cloves)
3	tablespoons chopped parsley

Preheat the oven to 350°F.

Heat 2 tablespoons of the oil in a large skillet. Dredge the lamb lightly in the flour and, in 2 or 3 batches, brown it on all sides.

In a separate large stew pot, cook the onion in the remaining table-spoon of the oil with the sage. Add the meat, wine, and salt and pepper. Cook over high heat until the wine has almost evaporated. In a small bowl, dissolve the tomato paste in the beef broth. When the wine has boiled away, stir in the broth and cover the pot tightly.

Bake the stew for 1½ hours. Add the beans and cook for another 15 minutes. Stir in the garlic and parsley and serve.

MOM'S SPAGHETTI SAUCE

makes about 2 quarts

I have very clear memories of eating this sauce cold right from the refrigerator the next day, I loved it so much as a child. It's a hit with my kids today. The celery and onions are pureed so the kids won't pick them out. Don't go for the leanest meat; you'll sacrifice flavor. I divide this recipe into three gallon-size sealable plastic bags and store them in the freezer for instant meals. Send it to the neighbors with a box of spaghetti, or cook the noodles and stir in the sauce. Include a loaf of garlic bread, a package of salad greens, and dinner's set.

2 tablespoons olive oil

1 1/2 cups coarsely chopped onion

1 cup chopped celery, including leafy sections

2 or 3 garlic cloves, minced (1 to 1 1/2 teaspoons)

2 teaspoons dried basil

1 pound ground beef

2 (20-ounce) cans tomato puree

4 or 5 beef bouillon cubes

Heat the oil in a large stew pot. Add the onions, celery, and garlic, and sauté them over medium-high heat until they're completely transparent, about 10 minutes. Transfer the mixture to a food processor, add the basil, and pulse until it's pureed.

In the same pot, brown the beef, breaking up any chunks with a wooden spoon. The longer you brown the meat the more flavorful the sauce will be. Add the tomato puree, the onion and celery mixture, and the bouillon cubes. (Do not add salt; the cubes are salty enough.)

Bring the sauce to a simmer, and cook for 1 hour, stirring occasionally. Serve it immediately, or divide it into 3 portions and freeze for up to 3 months.

illness
when it's a long haul

If a neighbor or family faces a long battle for recovery, there are lots of different ways for the neighborhood to pitch in. It's natural to want to make a helping gesture as soon as you hear the news, but often the offers slow to a trickle when the initial shock of concern has faded. Chances are it's the support that comes in week three—or thirty—that will be appreciated and remembered most.

Here are things you can *continue* to do:

- Provide meals, even if only occasionally
- Invite the rest of the family over for dinner; it breaks the difficult routine
- Make regular library or video-rental runs
- Baby-sit
- Offer to grocery shop for the family
- Bring by magazines or paperback books
- Help with transportation
- Cut the grass
- Shovel the sidewalk
- Bring the newspaper inside
- Walk the dog

Stay in for the long haul. People who face months of medical procedures or bed rest must not only battle for their health, they must also battle tedium, loneliness, and sometimes depression. Invite yourself to lunch, and bring all the fixings. My mother had major foot surgery that left her bedridden for four months. Not a weekday went by that she didn't have a chum make an appointment to visit. My dad could go to work and not worry that she was alone all day. They always arrived with a delicious lunch and many brought enough for dinner so that my dad had a good meal when he got home. Their generosity and commitment to my mother impressed us all, but it didn't surprise us; and they simply continued to treat her as a neighbor and dear friend.

If you do intend to bring lunch, store-bought or homemade, be sure to make it convenient. There shouldn't be any cleanup work or storage issues. And call ahead with your intentions. But do call.

MOM'S BEEF STEW

makes 6 to 8 servings

This has been a household favorite for thirty-five years. My mother still brings this dish to her neighbors, and it is always gratefully received.

- 2 pounds beef stew meat
- 1 tablespoon vegetable oil
- 2 tablespoons flour
- 3 garlic cloves
- 1 teaspoon salt
- 1/2 teaspoon dried thyme
- 2 tablespoons chopped fresh parsley
- 1 big bay leaf
- 1 cup dry red wine
- 2 cups beef broth
- 6 large russet potatoes, peeled and cut into chunks
- 3 yellow onions, quartered
- 6 carrots, cut into chunks

Preheat the oven to 325°F.

Pat the beef dry with paper towels. Heat the oil in a large skillet over medium-high heat and brown the meat on all sides. Place the meat in a heavy 4-quart Dutch oven.

Sprinkle the flour over the meat. Mash the garlic, and add it to the pan, along with the remaining ingredients. Cover, and bake until the beef and potatoes are tender, about 2 hours.

Adjust the seasonings, and serve the stew hot over noodles or biscuits.

ROAST CHICKEN AND CHICKEN GRAVY

makes 4 to 6 servings

So many people seem intimidated about making gravy. But in fact, it is extremely easy and has a flavor you cannot find in a jar. Just use the fat and delicious drippings that accumulate when you roast the bird, and you're home free.

1 whole chicken

Kosher salt

2 tablespoons butter

Canned chicken broth if necessary

2 tablespoons flour

Salt and freshly ground pepper to taste

Preheat the oven to 400°F.

Rinse the chicken, and pat it dry. Generously salt the cavity, and rub butter on the outside of the bird. Place the chicken in the center of a large roasting pan. Roast it for 1½ to 2 hours, depending on the size, or until the leg moves freely and the internal temperature reaches 170°F on an instant-read thermometer.

Remove the roasted chicken from the pan, and place it on a cutting board. Cover loosely with foil. Pour all the pan juices into a measuring cup. Spoon off 2 tablespoons of the fat from the drippings, and return them to the roasting pan. Skim off the remaining fat and discard. Add chicken broth to the pan juices if needed to make 1 cup.

Turn the heat to low and place the roasting pan on the heat. Gradually sprinkle in the 2 tablespoons of flour over the 2 tablespoons of chicken fat, whisking the mixture. Continue to whisk, scraping the pan for any extra cooked bits of chicken, for at least 2 minutes. The mixture should be a thick paste. Slowly mix in the reserved pan juices from the measuring cup. Continue to stir until the liquid has thickened into a nice gravy. Season to taste with salt and pepper.

One New Year's Eve, Janet Dohoney and her neighbors and friends decided to get all dressed up and stay home. The reason was simple. Janet's dear friend Barbara Person was just coming off chemotherapy and was understandably tired. She wasn't up for going out in public, even for New Year's.

Janet went all out — decorating her house, picking up noisemakers and silly hats. She pushed the furniture back in her living room and set up a few tables for the sixteen people she was expecting.

To make the evening a treat for everyone — even the hostess — Janet had the meal catered. Since one of the neighbors at the party had the best view to see the local fireworks display, everyone walked down the street to her house to watch the show and have champagne. And then it was back to Janet's for coffee and dessert.

How did Barbara react to all of this? "Janet has been such a good friend to me. She organized friends and neighbors to help drive me to and from my treatments, which were an hour and fifteen minutes away — each way . . . for a month straight! So often people who are sick don't talk about it, and they end up suffering alone in silence. Spending New Year's Eve with friends and neighbors was a wonderful way to ring in the new year."

MASHED POTATOES

mashed
potatoes

makes 8 to 10 servings

Next to chicken soup, mashed potatoes may just be the world's favorite comfort dish. Here is a recipe that freezes, too, thanks to the cream cheese. Roast a chicken, make the gravy and mashed potatoes, and you have a meal no family would turn down.

8 russet potatoes

1 teaspoon salt

6 tablespoons (³/₄ stick) butter

1 cup milk

4 ounces cream cheese, cut into cubes

Rinse and peel the potatoes, and cut them into thirds. Place them in a deep pan, cover them with water, and add the salt. Cook over medium heat until the potatoes can be pierced easily with a fork.

In a glass bowl or measuring cup, microwave the butter and milk together on HIGH for 45 seconds, or until very warm.

Drain the potatoes, and return them to low heat for just a moment; you want them to dry out without burning. Remove the potatoes from the heat, and mash them well in the pan. Slowly pour in the milk and butter, a third of the liquid at a time, and continue mashing the potatoes well at the same time. Stir in the cream cheese, and blend. Serve the potatoes hot, or freeze and reheat them.

FRENCH-ROASTED PARSNIP
AND CARROT STICKS

parsnip
carrot sticks

makes 8 servings

Send this over with a roast chicken to a neighbor in need. It's easy and tastes excellent.

8 carrots

8 parsnips

3 tablespoons extra virgin olive oil

Sea salt

Preheat the oven to 450°F.

Cut the carrots and parsnips into 2-inch-long sections. Cut the sections in half and then into quarters so that they are all roughly the same size.

Place the vegetables in a bowl, and toss them with the olive oil.

Arrange the carrots and parsnips on a cookie sheet, in a single layer. Sprinkle them with salt. Roast the sticks for 25 minutes, turning them occasionally.

impossible times

In many neighborhoods when someone dies, a reception following the funeral or memorial service is held at the family's home, but it is entirely organized by neighbors, from setup to cleanup. What a thoughtful tradition. If it is an option, consider taking this up in your area. It can be such a relief for the family.

Consider some other ideas in times of bereavement:

- Comfort food—the actress Dixie Carter once wrote that her mother always kept a chocolate cake in the fridge for such occasions. Frozen cookie dough can be baked up quickly, too.

- If people are coming in from out of town for the service, offer to put up as many as you can accommodate. It will be so much more convenient than a hotel even two miles away. Remember those people need to be fed, too.

- Ask if any out-of-town guests need transportation.

- On the day of the service, offer to house-sit.

Finally, don't forget the bereaved person. Loss lingers, but it never dies. People who have lost someone—a sibling, a parent, a child—carry with them a grief that is hard to talk about. Knowing there are others who remember what they've lost and who care can be truly helpful. If someone near to you has suffered a loss, make a note of the anniversary. A visit or call near the date can be a real comfort.

When the mother of two young toddlers lost her battle with breast cancer, the neighbors stepped in immediately with meals and sitters. Soon the young girls' grandmother moved in to take care of them. A group of neighbors, recognizing that it's a challenge for anyone to keep little ones entertained, took turns creating craft bags for the girls. Every few days, two resealable plastic bags were dropped off at the house, loaded with everything the girls would need to complete the enclosed craft project.

when there is conflict

No neighborhood can expect to exist without experiencing its share of disagreements. Some can involve lots of neighbors; some can be a feud between two. There is no point pretending conflict doesn't and won't exist. How the neighborhood manages it is what matters.

The good news is that when a neighborhood has had fun together as a group, put faces to names, and spent time together, the conflicts that do arise are handled with less misunderstanding and tension. One of the most common sources of tension is an "improvement" that one neighbor makes to his home or property that impacts or affects another. A tree is cut down that offered shade to someone else. A second-floor addition blocks someone's view. A new air-conditioning unit makes more noise than it should, rumbling into another neighbor's tranquil backyard.

If you are going to do any work on your house or property that could in any way affect your neighbors, make them aware ahead of time. You may have the legal right to build a garage right next to his patio, but why let him discover the situation when the lumber company shows up? If you can, give neighbors a chance to absorb your plans. Take a moment to tell your contractor that you want him to be as respectful as possible during the work period and to abide by any town rules governing when a crew can begin to bang and when they must stop. Let neighbors know that if they have concerns about how construction is impacting their lives, they should call you. Sometimes a minor adjustment to the work being done can make a real difference to your neighbor, and making them part of the process rather than expecting them to live with the results can head disagreements off at the pass.

Chronic problems can be tougher. A neighbor habitually blares loud music. Someone constantly parks in front of your house. A dog is allowed to bark through the day or night. Below are a few annoying habits. If you recognize yourself in them, consider a change.

- Sidewalks that don't get thoroughly shoveled — this can be a legal liability, too.

- Garage area left to look like a dump

- Dog allowed off the leash

- Porch and garage lights that glare into bedrooms overnight

- Kids that drive too fast through the neighborhood

- You drive too fast through the neighborhood

- Unsightly junk allowed to pile up in the front or backyard

- Letting bushes overgrow into the neighbor's yard

- Mowing the lawn on weekends before 9:00 A.M.

- Not ever mowing the lawn

Asking neighbors to change is hard. While you may want to discuss your options with other neighbors, fight the temptation to get a group riled up or ganging up against a single neighbor. It is important to keep emotions low and the number of concerned people to only those directly affected.

Some people avoid confrontation at all costs. Others get a real charge out of collecting problems until there's no seeing reason. Neither of these tactics is effective.

Here are some ideas for resolving conflicts:

- Keep different disagreements separate. One neighbor may do a few things that bug you. Don't let each pile up into an emotional hate fest.

- Make certain you are right. If it's a noise issue, does the town have guidelines?

- Is it really chronic, or only an occasional offense that you could actually live with?

- Try writing a brief handwritten note. It may be the first time a neighbor becomes aware there is a problem. Reading it gives them time to think through their own opinion before having to respond.

- Generous actions can go a long way, but when all else fails, decide how you are going to live with the situation without it ruining neighborhood solidarity.

An old house we lived in was sanded and painted one summer. Just as it was nearing completion, we got a call from the Environmental Protection Agency saying they needed to come test our home to see if we had deposited any harmful chemicals in the process. We had used professionals and were certain we hadn't, but an anonymous neighbor had put the call in. We were so disappointed that there was a neighbor in our area who did not feel comfortable enough to call us first. What do you do? We decided to draft a letter that was as open and straightforward as possible and that included the good findings by the EPA, and gave a copy to every neighbor. Oddly enough, we had many neighbors stop us to apologize that someone would call anonymously.

when to call the cops

Let's face it, truly life-threatening events can take place in any neighborhood. Sometimes the really caring thing to do is step in and get real help:

- If you are an eyewitness to physical abuse to a child, an animal, or an adult. It's called battery. It's a crime.
- If you hear screams for help, even if you can't pinpoint the location, call. You could save a life.
- If you observe a marked decline in the function of an older neighbor, who seems confused or looks disheveled; if the grass suddenly isn't cut, or the newspapers stack up and the car's in the driveway, perhaps a family member needs to be called. Dementia, Alzheimer's disease, and other devastating mental problems can be hidden from view until a person's life is at risk. If there is no family, today's police are trained to assess such situations. Don't be embarrassed to call in a professional.

When Linda's "oddball" neighbor, a diagnosed paranoid schizophrenic, cut off his utilities in winter, quit eating anything but carrots, and retreated into his demons, his neighbors were at a loss for what to do. Linda had taken food to him for years—extra soup, bread, or half a cake. But now, when she peered through the front window and saw him curled up in a sleeping bag on the living room floor on a subfreezing day, she threw up her hands and called his mother, who brought in the authorities and had the man hospitalized. His medications were stabilized, and the last Linda heard, he had a job spinning classical records late at night at the local public radio station. Without that intervention, he would have been dead. It was a tough call, but a necessary one.

a gift of friendship

Recently I drove for three hours in the pouring rain to spend a short afternoon with my old friend Margaret Fitzgerald. Her brother had died recently, and her husband called me to say Margaret was in deep despair. I know that visit meant a lot to her, but I think it may have meant even more to me.

Margaret Fitzgerald moved into my old neighborhood about six months after we did. At the time I was into making strawberry jam, and I left a jar at the front door to welcome them. Some time later my husband, Todd, and I were sitting on our old screened porch and we heard footsteps on the driveway. It was Margaret, still dressed in work clothes and heels, stopping by to say thanks for the jam. She stayed for over an hour, and we had a delightful, funny conversation. For five years Margaret, Tom, and their kids were our neighbors. Along with a few other families, we shared everything—tools, meals, bath time, holidays, recipes, and great times. Not all neighbors become best friends, but this group did. I have lived in three neighborhoods since then, and in each, I have come to value the comfort, fun, and support of what it means to live in a neighborhood and be a neighbor. I've made dear friends, and I've come to know interesting and remarkable people.

Hokey as it may sound, the experience has brought home the lesson that it is not the destination that matters at all. It is the journey—and the journey is much, much better when you're not alone!

share your success

I'd love to hear the stories of your neighborhood and what works for you.

From small acts of kindness to parties, themes, and events—what makes your neighborhood special?

E-mail me at: Peggy@Allen.net

index

conversion chart
Equivalent Imperial and Metric Measurements

American cooks use standard containers, the 8-ounce cup and a tablespoon that takes exactly 16 level fillings to fill that cup level. Measuring by cup makes it very difficult to give weight equivalents, as a cup of densely packed butter will weigh considerably more than a cup of flour. The easiest way therefore to deal with cup measurements in recipes is to take the amount by volume rather than by weight. Thus the equation reads:

1 cup = 240 ml = 8 fl. oz.   ½ cup = 120 ml = 4 fl. oz.

It is possible to buy a set of American cup measures in major stores around the world.

In the States, butter is often measured in sticks. One stick is the equivalent of 8 tablespoons. One tablespoon of butter is therefore the equivalent to ½ ounce/15 grams.

Liquid Measures

Fluid U.S. Ounces		Imperial	Milliliters
	1 teaspoon	1 teaspoon	5
¼	2 teaspoons	1 dessertspoon	10
½	1 tablespoon	1 tablespoon	14
1	2 tablespoons	2 tablespoons	28
2	¼ cup	4 tablespoons	56
4	½ cup		110
5		¼ pint or 1 gill	140
6	¾ cup		170
8	1 cup		225
9			250, ¼ liter
10	1¼ cups	½ pint	280
12	1½ cups		340
15		¾ pint	420
16	2 cups		450
18	2¼ cups		500, ½ liter
20	2½ cups	1 pint	560
24	3 cups		675
25		1¼ pints	700
27	3½ cups		750
30	3¾ cups	1½ pints	840
32	4 cups or 1 quart		900
35		1¾ pints	980
36	4½ cups		1000, 1 liter
40	5 cups	2 pints or 1 quart	1120

Solid Measures

U.S. and Imperial Measures		Metric Measures	
Ounces	Pounds	Grams	Kilos
1		28	
2		56	
3½		100	
4	¼	112	
5		140	
6		168	
8	½	225	
9		250	¼
12	¾	340	
16			
	450		
18		500	½
20	1¼	560	
24	1½	675	
27		750	¾
28	1¾	780	
32	2	900	
36	2¼	1000	1
40	2½	1100	
48	3	1350	
54		1500	1½

Oven Temperature Equivalents

Fahrenheit	Celsius	Gas Mark	Description
225	110	¼	Cool
250	130	½	
275	140	1	Very Slow
300	150	2	
325	170	3	Slow
350	180	4	Moderate
375	190	5	
400	200	6	Moderately Hot
425	220	7	Fairly Hot
450	230	8	Hot
475	240	9	Very Hot
500	250	10	Extremely Hot

Any broiling recipes can be used with the grill of the oven, but beware of high-temperature grills.

Equivalents for Ingredients

all-purpose flour—plain flour
coarse salt—kitchen salt
cornstarch—cornflour
eggplant—aubergine

half and half—12% fat milk
heavy cream—double cream
light cream—single cream
lima beans—broad beans

scallion—spring onion
unbleached flour—strong, white flour
zest—rind
zucchini—courgettes or marrow